Cover image: TURTLAN by Cedric Price.

Edited by Samantha Hardingham

Essays by Simon Allford, Jane Briginshaw, Paul Finch, John Fraser, Jude Kelly, John Lyall, Robin Middleton, Kester Rattenbury, Neil Spiller, Robertson Ward Jr

Text by Samantha Hardingham and Cedric Price

Design by Mark Boyce

Published in Great Britain in 2003 by Wiley-Academy, a division of John Wiley & Sons Ltd
Reprinted May 2011

The Atrium, Southern Gate, Chichester, West Sussex PO19 8SQ, England
Telephone National 01243 779777
International (+44) 1243 779777
Email (for orders and customer service enquiries): cs-books@wiley.co.uk
Visit our Home Page on www.wileyeurope.com or www.wiley.com

Other Wiley Editorial Offices

John Wiley & Sons Inc., 111 River Street, Hoboken, NJ 07030, USA
Jossey-Bass, 989 Market Street, San Francisco, CA 94103-1741, USA
Wiley-VCH Verlag GmbH, Boschstr. 12, D-69469 Weinheim, Germany
John Wiley & Sons Australia Ltd, 33 Park Road, Milton, Queensland 4064, Australia
John Wiley & Sons (Asia) Pte Ltd, 2 Clementi Loop #02-01, Jin Xing Distripark, Singapore 129809
John Wiley & Sons Canada Ltd, 22 Worcester Road, Etobicoke, Ontario, Canada M9W 1L1

Wiley also publishes its books in a variety of electronic formats.
Some content that appears in print may not be available in electronic books.

ISBN 0470848758

Printed and bound in Italy

CEDRIC PRICE OPERA

EDITED BY SAMANTHA HARDINGHAM

WILEY-ACADEMY

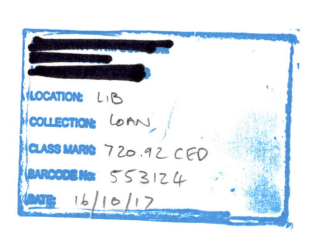

CONTENTS

——

INTRODUCTION

—

PRICE, Cedric J. Cedric John Price, eldest son of architect A.G.Price [1901-53] was born in Stone, Staffordshire, England in 1934. He studied architecture under John Penn [b.1921] at Cambridge University from 1952 to 1955, becoming President of the Cambridge University Society of Arts in 1954 and then attended the Architectural Association School from 1955 to 1957 where he studied under John Killick [1924-71]*. Price then worked for Fry, Drew and Partners and also worked on exhibition projects with Erno Goldfinger before setting up his own practice in 1960.[1]

*and perhaps more significantly, Arthur Korn (1891-1978), German architect, urban planner and teacher who worked with Erich Mendelsohn in Berlin and F.R.S. Yorke and E. Maxwell Fry in England. He was influential in urban planning circles as chairman (1938) of the MARS Town Planning Committee which was responsible for the Plan of London (1942).

Introduction.

Cedric Price likes books but he doesn't like making them – he is of the opinion that it takes too long and by the time one is produced it is out of date. The last and only book that he has helped to compile on the work of Cedric Price Architects (CPA) was in 1984 and entitled, *Cedric Price – Works II*. The book, was published by the Architectural Association specifically to accompany an exhibition of the practices' work in the same year (the 'Works II' relating to a series of books published by the AA at that time). It is the only comprehensive illustrated document of projects from 1960 – 1984. Throughout that period, and ever since then, tantalising pieces of Price's projects, writings and commentaries have appeared in a number of journals, the ephemeral nature of which suits and assists the critical underlying theme that runs through all of the projects: TIME, being the fourth dimension in design and Price's most treasured design tool.

The purpose of *Cedric Price Opera* is then to present a generous snapshot of the work of CPA carried out since 1985. Projects are arranged in sections devised by Price with his own leading notes at the beginning of each one outlining themes within the work-notes that were added to during the production of the book as ideas and opinions have changed over time. Different typefaces are used to help distinguish at a glance between Price's writings (set in the typewriter print characteristic of all CPA correspondence) and editorial description and captions. The text is peppered throughout with leads to further reading. In the same way that Price sees the city as "a wonderful place to pass through... a launching pad" (CITLIN), *Cedric Price Opera* serves as

a guide book. Duplication of previously published work has been avoided – unless, as Price states, "necessary repetition [is required] for the wilfully inattentive". Additional and invaluable contributions are made by a necessarily disparate group of Price's associates. One might call them comrades. The remit for these essays has been to explore the relevance, and importance of, Price's work in the context of 'now' from the point of view of amongst others, a client, an art historian, a journalist, a politician, an architect and an educator. Each one illuminates an aspect of either Price's method of working (see essays by Simon Allford, Jude Kelly, Jane Briginshaw and Paul Finch), or the themes within his work (see essays by John Lyall, Kester Rattenbury, John Frazer and Neil Spiller). Essays by Robin Middelton and Robertson Ward Jr together provide a sure foundation from which to explore the projects in more detail, each one providing a context which serve as fitting introductions in themselves.

The Situation is Now.

It is with the last point in mind that I write *this* introduction. The prime importance of being Cedric Price, architect, now is the high regard with which he holds both ideas and human beings. The depth and variety in the drawings alone are a testament to his personality; funny, poetic, explorative, optimistic, economical and always pertinent. His "boundless interest in life as observer and active participant in its richness, diversity, absurdity, misery and delight[1]" equips him with the information with which to construct his ideas, to communicate with his clients, friends and colleagues of any occupation, to tolerate members of his chosen profession and to field predators. The projects themselves are clear enough in their description of number, name, site and brief. But, from that point onwards it is the connections that are made by the participants and subsequently the viewers, and the questions that are asked by both that produce the proposals and begin to describe the continuity of changing pace that defines Price's unique insight and imagination.

Royston Landau[2] (also an invited contributor to this book but whose untimely death in 2001 occurred before a draft had been written) sites Price's major projects of the early years of the practice as the Aviary at London Zoo (1960), designed with Lord Snowdon and close associate and friend, engineer Frank Newby, The Fun Palace[3], east London (developed 1960-61) initiated with theatre director Joan Littlewood, the Potteries Thinkbelt[4], Staffordshire (1964-65), the built Inter-Action Centre, London (1971)[5] and Generator[6], U.S.A (1976). These are iconic projects both for Price and for the time, they are well published and references to them are listed at the back of the book. During this time Price also played a particularly active part in education (he continues to attend student presentations on a regular basis) and in developing new groups that "would be addressing new questions and new areas". The London Subterranean Survey Association (1969), The Quality of Life Commission (1970-78), the Lightweight Enclosure Unit (1969), and Polyark, the Architecture Schools Network Group (1971) are just some of the groups with which Price has associated himself, not to mention more elusive organisations such as the Hot Stuff Club and Gothic Film Club.

This range of interests and expertise is ever-expanding and the projects in this book illustrate that the office of CPA is not a place for stasis. It is impossible to crystallize Price or his work, past and present, in any 'era' or 'ism'. Landau goes on to describe that central to Price's ideology is "an indeterminate architecture, ...develop[ing] proposals always within a very precise and detailed context, so enabling the immediate and future consequences of the proposals to be closely examined... The connection between the complexities and potential of the question, and the physical (or nonphysical) end product, is very close, and because, like Buckminster Fuller, his work is consciously problem-solving and possessing almost no arbitrary formal allegiances, the importance of seeing each of his projects as a problem understanding and question-asking process..is necessary if it is to be understood."[7]. In his *Reyner Banham Lecture* of March 2001 Price said, "we must stop worrying about speaking the same language as one another but keep on thinking and speculating about the future." Titles of other lectures give more insight into the Pricean mode: "Future forecasting: Crystal balls – speculation into immediate futures"[8]; "Designing for Doubt, Delight and Demolition – the architect's duty to society".[9] Price's architecture is one of 'beneficial change', an 'anticipatory architecture' which argues that any built environment becomes inhibiting, restrictive, obsolete unless it can adapt to the yet-to-be-determined. The only sure thing is

that Time, and the duration of it, allows for change. He explores appropriate methods of construction and demolition in equal measure.

Artist Joseph Beuys used materials that were literally in a state of change. His sculptures were not conceived as fixed or finished pieces. Made from the stuff of life, with life; wool felt, lard, bones, honey, often partnered with or made into machines; using transmitters, batteries, magnets, torches and telephones. His performances provoked a change in condition, a surge of energy in order to stimulate continuous change. Real actions rather than interpretations. In his 'Manifesto on the foundation of a "Free International School for Creativity and Interdisciplinary Research", (written with Heinrich Boll in1973)[10] he states that "the chief goal [of the school] is the encouragement discovery and furtherance of democratic potential, and the expression of this." Compare this with either the excerpts from Price's National School Plan of 1964 in John Lyall's essay, or his MAGNET project. Unlike the Situationist International's Utopian quest to over-come nature by planning "complex and enormous spacex" and thus rather imperiously transforming society, for Beuys and Price "the situation is now[12]" and they both offer enabling skills to fellow citizens, rather than assuming the role of dictator or teacher. As Price puts it, "its about where you decide to position yourself", again emphasising the high regard with which he holds client relationships and "the most delicate flowers of all, people"[13].

Price has an insatiable appetite and unwavering commitment to accruing (listening and finding), processing (drawing) and imparting (talking and proposing) information. In any other field this might be called research in its widest and most exhilarating sense and would be respected, supported and remunerated accordingly. But, in architecture these activities are absurdly regarded as somewhat of a 'charming' indulgence to the 'reality' of what Price calls, "the enclosure business". It is the very same 'reality' that Price has been so bold and brave in suspending which allows all possibilities to remain

gloriously open. Alistair McAlpine once quoted, in reference to his good friend Cedric, that "a prophet is never without honour except in his own country".[14] In this context I would liken Price's assessment of the architectural profession to that of artist, Barnett Newman's opinion of the Surrealists, "they practiced illusion because they did not feel the magic"[15].

Meanwhile Price is unerred. After more than 40 years in practice Price continues to ask questions and "make tireless efforts towards dignifying life generally"[16]. The chapter headings in this book ask a few questions, particularly of the current ease with which we use words such as 'sustainability', 'regeneration', 'brownfield site', 'density', 'identity', 'bridge', 'shelter', what constitutes 'best practice', how do we 'rethink construction'? His is "The Harvest of the Quiet Eye"[17]. And we would all do well to listen. It is quiet though, so you have to listen carefully.

Samantha Hardingham - March 2003

Note about abbreviations in this book:
CPA – Cedric Price Architects
CP – Cedric Price
BD – Building Design
AJ - Architect's Journal
AA – Architectural Association School of Architecture

I would like to thank CP and all the contributors for giving their time.

1 – GREEN

"NEVER THINK OF A SURFACE EXCEPT AS A VOLUME"
HENRY MOORE

NEW 'FREE' WATER	NEW WATER	PERIPHERAL WATERS	EXISTING 'FREE' WATER	NEW CONTROLLED WATER
196 DUCKLANDS	213 MARSHAM ST	178 JAPNET 201 TURTLAN	199 SURF	212 MILLS
				181 SERRE I 189 SERRE II

DEMOLITION — MINIMUM DISTURBANCE — VARIED DISCONTINUOUS STRUCTURES INCLUDING BRIDGES — TUBULAR STRUCTURE

SAME SHAPE – DIFFERENT SCALE

PUBLIC/RESIDENTS – NEW, RE-USAGE — PUBLIC USE – RESIDENTS & VISITORS — PUBLIC INFORMATION & DELIGHT

CITY LUNG — TERRAIN RELIEF — PART OF A BIGGER PUBLIC PARK

DEMOLISH FOR NEW — INVISIBLE TUNING-UP — ROUTES / STONES / WATERS — IN/OUT / 2 BITS / 3 BITS + WATER

CHANGE THROUGH TIME — INFORMATION – FLOW – MOVEMENT — THE ADDATIVE QUALITY OF THE FLOWING RIVER — GROWING THINGS / MAKING THINGS / THE PRODUCTION FLOOR

AGEING — EXCHANGE – NATURE OF EXCHANGE / TOURISM – CHANGE OF LOCALE / DELIGHT – IN EXCHANGE — THE SITING OF THINGS WHICH RELATE TO A RIVER — RELATING THE POSITION OF THE MAKING OF THINGS TO THE ARCHITECTURAL SITING OF THE "PRODUCTION FLOOR"

CHANGE IN LOCAL GROWTH — LOCALE – OF DELIGHT / LOCALE – DELIGHT — THE ACTION OF WATER / TIDAL EFFECTS

THE HUMAN DELIGHT IN WATER, IN TIDES — THE SITING OF THE ONE CONTRASTING WITH THE OTHER

IN THE TIMING OF TIDES

HUMAN DELIGHT – IN TIMING / CELEBRATION – TOURISM / TIMING – FLOW — THE CITY GREENHOUSE / THE COUNTRY GREENHOUSE / GROWING ROSES / MAKING PERFUME FROM ROSES

1–
GREEN

181/189
SERRE I/II

181 SERRE I is a proposal for a greenhouse located in the Parc de la Villette in Paris, north of the canal de l'Ourcq and adjacent to the lock on the canal de St. Denis.

Having produced the initial scheme, the following excerpts are taken from a "second stage" report produced by CPA for perfume manufacturer, Derly, who became the main client for the project called 189 SERRE II. The revised scheme, a commercial property for the growing and exhibiting of roses, has to accommodate a shift in client's demand; an increased business of plan caused it to be "bursting at its seams".

The building (a 'secret garden' in contrast to the public park) required two distinct active zones. The one is a habitable greenhouse where spectacular plants form a permanent setting for exhibitions and social events. The other is a series of volumes providing facilities for meetings, research, administration and servicing. The whole building is enriched by the scent, colours and texture of the varied plants and the sound of falling water. Investigations were undertaken to achieve a maximum internal volume consistent with the obtaining of the maximum natural light.

The building is designed to ensure that the total volume (internally) is immediately comprehensible. However, the complexity and variety of the planting takes time to explore. The internal structures are all designed to adapt to change of both usage and occupancy. The concrete decks supported on columns enable re-organisation of sizes and usage of total areas. The walkways, being both lightweight and self-supporting, can be realigned.

The introduction of the red London bus on drawings is increasingly useful to us as designers - the stamp [when placed on a drawing] realises the openness we want to achieve as prescribed by the scale. It introduces urban constrictions of siting and operation.

This building is literally green = growth, not green = social do-goodery. A greenhouse depends on the sun. It is not a justification for it.

Reading List - *Vole* was the first UK Green magazine and I read every issue with the mental enjoyment equivalent to that engendered physically by the scratching of a scab... Now, some years later, its editor Richard North has written a book, *Life on a Modern Planet - Manifesto for Progress*. I think it rather jolly and regret the current Green Jacket reaction. Read it. Together with Will Hutton's book *The State We're In* - I wish I'd thought of that title! I don't know why I've plugged these books, apart from liking public libraries. I once bought alot of ex-stock from Ludlow Public Library; I think it was closing. Price Probes, BD, 3 March 1995

Ref: Vaisseau de Pierre 2, "Parc Ville Villette", Champ Vallon, 1987.
Ref: Paul Finch, "Time to Take Stock", BD, 11 March 1994.

SERRE

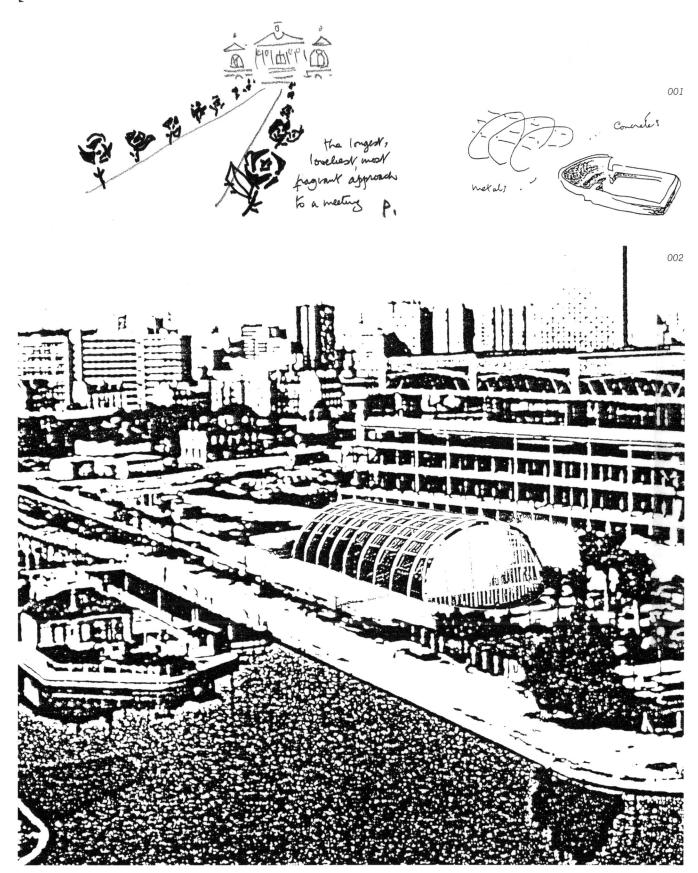

the longest, loveliest, most fragrant approach to a meeting P.

metals

Concrete?

001

002

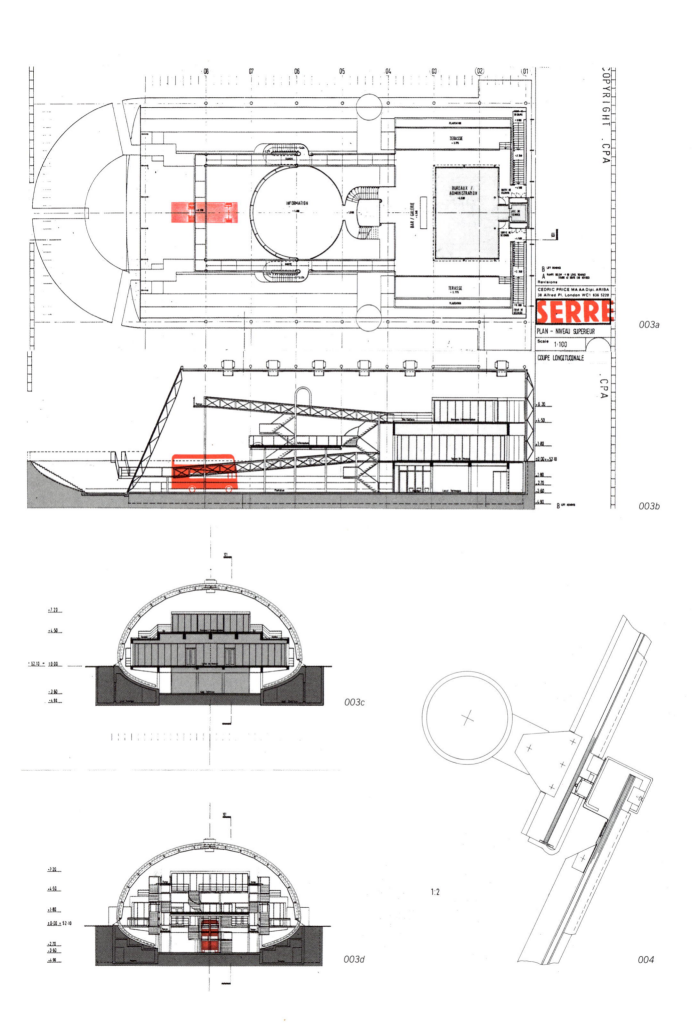

003a

003b

003c

003d

004

1:2

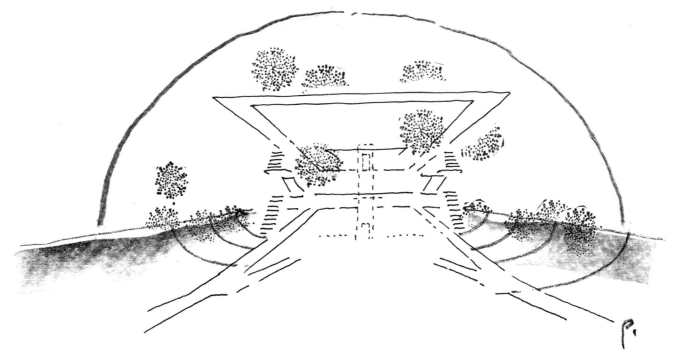

looking NORTH - from low level

SERRE

005a

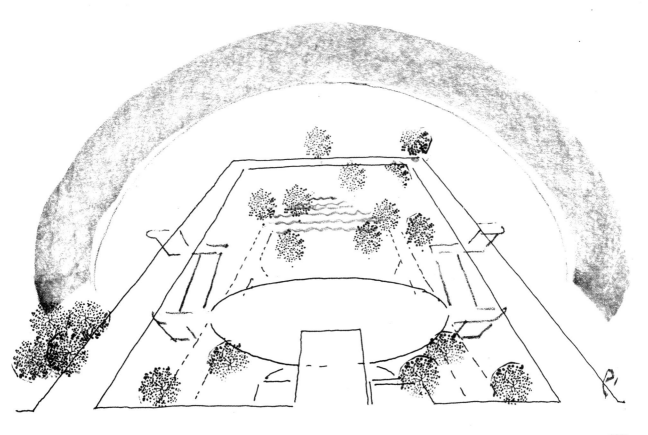

005b

looking SOUTH - from high level.

212
MILLS

The site is Mill Meads, East London located close to both the intended site of the Fun Palace and due south of 190 STRATE. Pedestrian riverside movement is combined with phased agronomy and a public space programme.

In acknowledgement of the importance of a major London river, the River Lea and its tributries the Channelsea and Mills Wall Rivers, CPA have introduced on-site footpaths, walkways and bridges to enable safe pedestrian movement at will on all routes throughout 24 hours and in all seasons. However, these devices are secondary to the secret but inherent, powerful and all pervading movement of water. All interventions are accepting of the fact that the movement of water and its capacity to be cleaned and controlled are to be respected.

The form and detail of bridges, quays and promenades enable them to undertake and provide various additional tasks and services, e.g.

Bridges: water control and monitoring.

Quays: water craft anchorage, bank maintenance.

Promenades: good viewing and safe congregation.

A report compiled by CPA for client, Union Rail includes the implementation of the following measures:

- the opening up and restoration of lengths of the Channelsea River accelerating the formation of the renewed river bed by installing river fountains (a water clock).
- the showcasing of industries and activities alongside the long established commercial and industrial base in the area, thus enabling phased shared servicing.
- the installation of sentinel towers as major visual and organizational site fixes.
- purification of the land, planting and husbandry.
- power and information sources to enable seemingly impossible events to occur with small individual capital costs and short preparation times.
- all the 'crops' will be selected for seasonal colours and odour whilst providing friendly barriers to otherwise hostile terrain.
- the site must never look neglected or incomplete however little built environment exists.

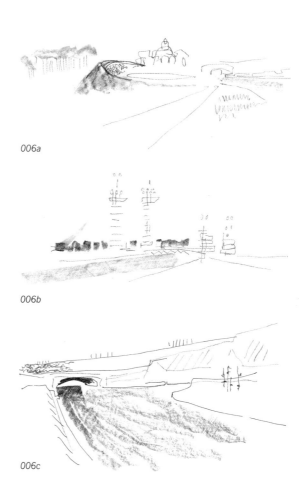

006a

006b

006c

This page:
006a, b, c. various sketch proposal views
of Mill Meads.
Opposite:
007. photocopy of map with key waterways
on site marked in black.

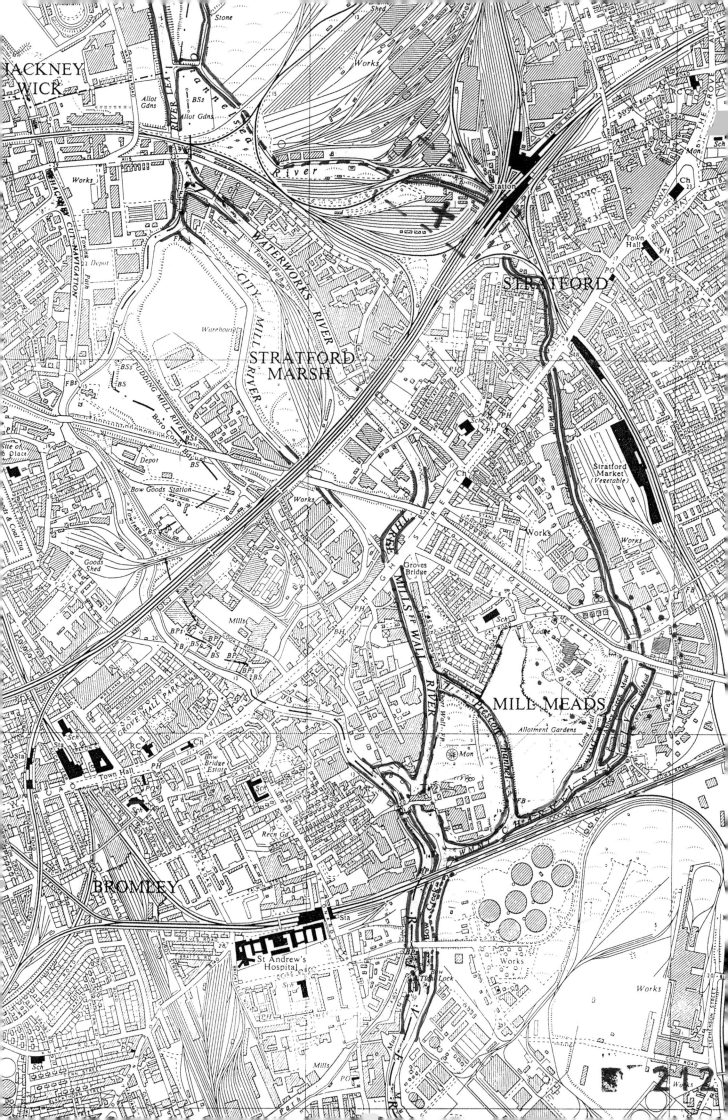

199
SURF '90

A competition entry for Sagami Bay,
south of Tokyo; a large pleasure beach
in Japan.

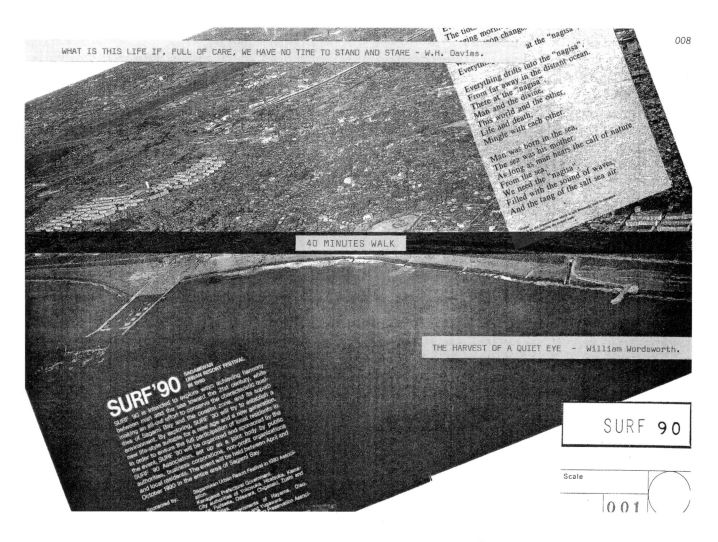

This page:
008. title page for SURF '90 competition entry.
Pages 018, 019:
*009a, b, c, d, e, f, g, h. pages with detailed notes
on each drawing from SURF '90 proposal document.*

Sagami Bay is, like all magic objects - so valuable that it must be used. It both supports and enhances human life - this peculiar enrichment is of both body and spirit. These proposals suggest that the most valuable gift of Sagami Bay to those that live here and those who visit is one of TIME.

To this end, all the strategies, tactics and artifacts proposed are viewed as making a particular, recognisable alteration in one's attitude to both free-will and controlled time - that is both 'leisure' & 'work' time. These present day definitions are redundant. All time is equally precious to the spirit and its use should be of constant pleasure. Modern man has not realised this fully and therefore 'spends' time rather than 'using' it. The mobile or static state consumes the same amount of time in the journey of the mind.

The strategy is to establish a capacity for responsive change so that the future value of the plan will be realised. The tactics of the plan contain land usage proposals, invisible communication provisions and the design and installation of particular structures both mobile and static.

There is a pressure on land. People, movement, pressure, green - real green.

The generators of tourism are the desire for pleasure, curiosity, uniqueness and difficulty of achievement. Thus this unpaid labour force of millions accepting few limits either on nationality, race or creed is likely to pay money and attention to areas, objects and methods for the passing of time that are viewed in a very different light by those in paid employ.

However, not only are both groups frequently the same people with only a time difference but the difference between validity of the place or process for these two groups is found in an increasingly small time span.

Tourism is becoming a regular event for most in the developed and developing countries of the world - whether confined to the native country or not. In the same way activital patterning recognised as 'work' can simultaneously be seen as 'leisure' when observed, rather than indulged in, elsewhere.

Thus tourism is no longer the rich looking in wonder at the poor, or the past, more a continuing appetite for the determining where, what and why is the difference in contemporary life patterning. This vast and stable industry, highly profitable to its host nation, requires more than well-maintained relics of the past: it requires, in fact, physical means to achieve pleasurable recognition and understanding of the present and the future.

Methods for such acheivement and their resultant physical effect on natural and man-made environments must become a major element in future land use planning.

Such provision at initial stages of new or altered development - physical or operational - can be a major design task that can enhance environment far more than the particular considerations at present allow to individual activities.

We cannot be slovenly about assumptions. I like the pressure for the entire office that requires all of us to rethink the basics. CP April 1979.

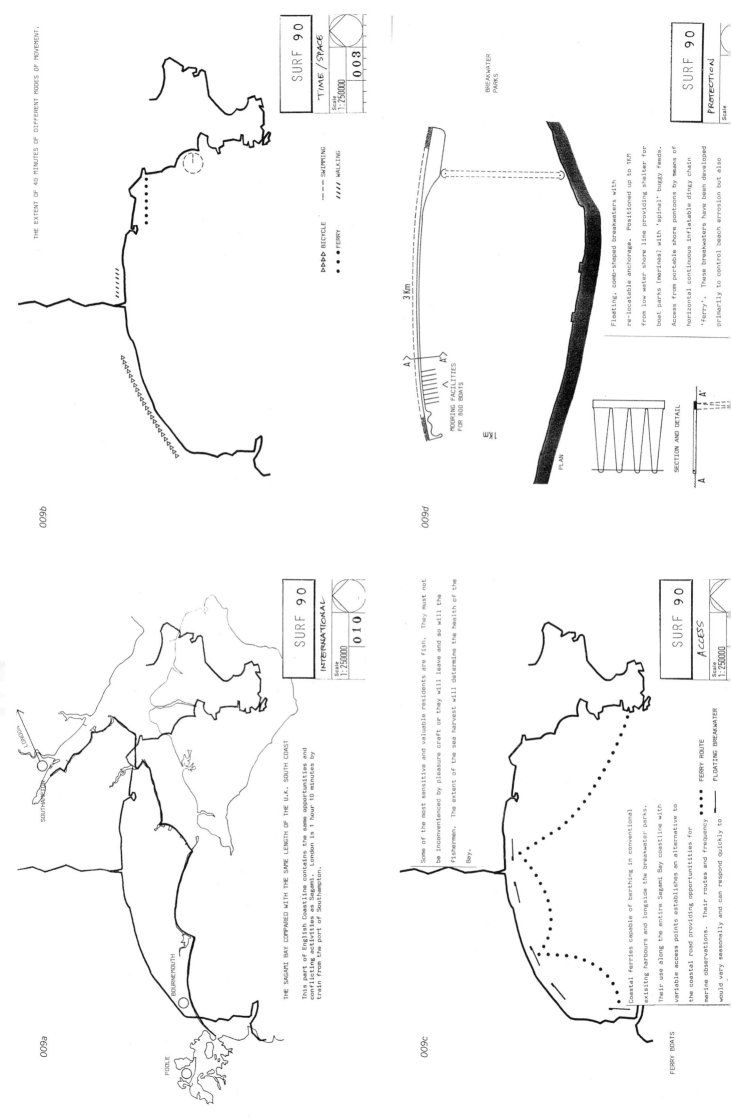

009b

THE EXTENT OF 40 MINUTES OF DIFFERENT MODES OF MOVEMENT.

▷▷▷▷ BICYCLE — — SWIMMING

● ● ● FERRY //// WALKING

SURF 90

TIME/SPACE

Scale 1:250000

003

009d

BREAKWATER PARKS

3 Km

MOORING FACILITIES FOR 800 BOATS

1Km

PLAN

SECTION AND DETAIL

A' A

Floating, comb-shaped breakwaters with re-locatable anchorage. Positioned up to 1KM from low water shore line providing shelter for boat parks (marinas) with 'spinal' buggy feeds. Access from portable shore pontoons by means of horizontal continuous inflatable dingy chain 'ferry'. These breakwaters have been developed primarily to control beach errosion but also

SURF 90

PROTECTION

Scale

009a

LONDON

SOUTHAMPTON

BOURNEMOUTH

POOLE

THE SAGAMI BAY COMPARED WITH THE SAME LENGTH OF THE U.K. SOUTH COAST

This part of English Coastline contains the same opportunities and conflicting activities as Sagami. London is 1 hour 10 minutes by train from the port of Southampton.

SURF 90

INTERNATIONAL

Scale 1:250000

010

009c

Some of the most sensitive and valuable residents are fish. They must not be inconvenienced by pleasure craft or they will leave and so will the fishermen. The extent of the sea harvest will determine the health of the Bay.

FERRY BOATS   Coastal ferries capable of berthing in conventional exisiting harbours and longside the breakwater parks. Their use along the entire Sagami Bay coastline with variable access points establishes an alternative to the coastal road providing opportunitities for marine observations. Their routes and frequency would vary seasonally and can respond quickly to

●●●● FERRY ROUTE

—— FLOATING BREAKWATER

SURF 90

ACCESS

Scale 1:250000

009f

Tokyo is extremely fortunate to have so close a 'lung' as Sagami Bay. The residents are enriched by this neighbouring giant. All must realise the dynamic nature of this relationship and its likelihood of continuous change.

The precious quality of the physical fabric, land and sea is the responsibility of all. The seasons are the surest agents of change

EXISTING RAIL NETWORK

⊕ 35,000 - 60,000
◉ 10,000 - 35,000
○ UP TO - 10,000

◈ RENEWAL CASKETS

	SURF 90
PASSENGERS	
Scale 1:250000	009

SAFETY THRESHOLDS

These consist of a pedestrian 'boardwalk' spread over transportable lightweight bridging structures capable of spanning, for example, the coastal highway. These wide structures are for pedestrian and bicycle use only and introduce a safe double fan shaped threshold to both beach and hinterland.

009h

	SURF 90
SAFETY THRESHOLD	
Scale	016

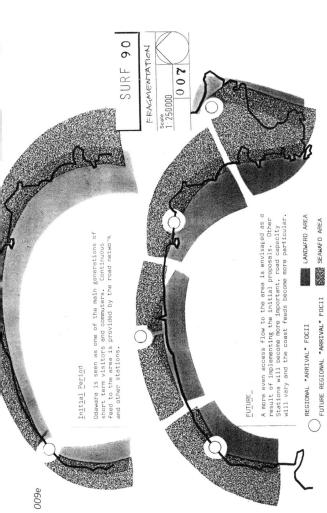

009e

Initial Period

Odawara is seen as one of the main generations of short term visitors and commuters. Continuous feed to the area is provided by the road network and other stations.

FUTURE

A more even access flow to the area is envisaged as a result of implementing the initial proposals. Other Stations will become more important, road capacity will vary and the coast feeds become more particular.

○ REGIONAL "ARRIVAL" FOCII
◉ FUTURE REGIONAL "ARRIVAL" FOCII

▪ LANDWARD AREA
▒ SEAWARD AREA

	SURF 90
FRAGMENTATION	
Scale 1:250000	007

RENEWAL CASKETS

These caskets would be located at and incorporated into the forecourt areas of stations, car-parks and other disembarkation points for visitors and commuters to the entire area. The caskets sometimes entire rooms sometimes a small shelter, a kiosk or a comfortable bench would, through their form, colour and positioning be readily visible to the stranger. The content of the caskets would vary with time but refreshment of mind and body would be their aim. Copious washing and toilet facilities, baby care and foot, eye and skin husbandry would be provided as would free local telephone calls and very light refreshments. The aim would be to produce a cleaner happier and more rested person than had arrived - whether from work or the beach. The community would be the 'host' - the visitor the grateful 'guest'.

009g

'Hello, Goodbye'
as spaces - variable
benches

- provide free
information / guidance
bag saving, telephones
rest - primarily they re-condition the
individual into their leaves the PARK. feeling.

better than before.

	SURF 90
AMENITY	
Scale	015

178
JAPNET

A competition for student housing in Kawasaki, Japan, designed in collaboration with cybernetician, Professor Gordon Pask.

Pask's sketches of complex feedback systems lay out a concept for a system of communications and information for the whole of Kawasaki as described in the adjacent notes. Price describes the area as a "community without propinquity". His vast grid of spheres (as multi-directional receptors, receivers and transmitters of mixed-media) are spread over the site and layered to form varying levels of exchange and a form of advanced information.

Price introduced Pask to architecture as consultant cybernetician during the very early stages of the development of FUN PALACE. Pask formed a Cybernetics Committee to act as a filter for ideas and discuss problems of cost and control. Members included Stafford Beer, Chester Beatty, Tom Driberg MP, Richard Gregory and of course Price and Littlewood.

Ref: **Joan's Book** for detailed list.

The Intelligent Plaza

There are distinct sketches (rough perspectives and sections) for the other than dynamic component of an exhibit; the Architecture of Knowledge. The topology is theoretically valid and these are some of the "basic forms" (or "fundamental elements") of such a structure. In combination with many others of the same kind they should represent the thoughts of the city and a computer-animated image of the built structure may evolve. The structure itself may, perhaps, be supported by a minimally built tensionally integral space-frame to emphasise the global unity of thought and its local idiosyncrasies. The structure is complementary to an also theoretically defensible but, as yet, less developed kinetics to be represented by animation of the (sculptural physical) structure and its evolution (for example, proposals for city development) by computer graphics also in the plaza.

Representation of a concept. Process of concept application is complementary (inside directional line) to the torroidal carapace (the structure distinguishing the concept). Its existence generates, under coherence (hermanutic) (sic) and distinction logic (with process interpretation) a distinguishing or repellent force.

Notes written by Pask and attached to working drawings.

The invisible postman; all that is available in accepted forms of socio/municipal exchange made available for random access/use in areas relevantly used for other reasons.

Ref. Munich Olympic Village, Cedric Price Architects.

This page:
010. the 24-hour postman.
Opposite (left hand column - drawings by CP):
011. photocopy collage showing location and scale
of information spheres on site.
012. sketch of information spheres.
013. sketch plan and section of position
of spheres across site.
Opposite (right hand column - drawings by GP):
014. flow of information in space.
015. representation of a concept - see notes.
016. Kawasaki Suspension- see notes
'The Intelligent Plaza'.

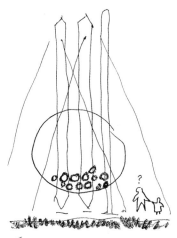

The 24-hour POSTMAN   010

011

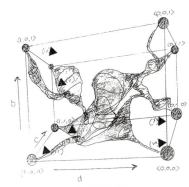

014

HI-LEVEL

Spheres as multi-directional
receptors & receivers of mixed media-transmits

LO-LEVEL

TV screens
Audio & speakers

012

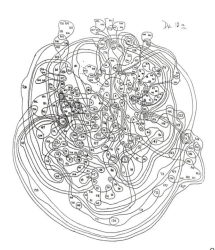

015

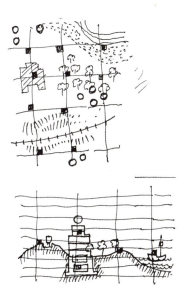

013

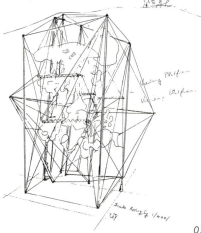

016

201
TURTLAN

The location is an artist's colony in the hilltown of Groznjan, former Yugoslavia. Price spent 10 days of 'Work Games' here at the 2nd International Symposium for Theory and Design in the Third Machine Age.

Price used this site as the basis for a competition entry (for Japanese A+U magazine) addressing the introduction of new communications into ancient sites; the addition of a force-field or halo around the village would eliminate the necessity to build new roads or dismantle existing structures - a response that was inspired by the physical peculiarity of the hill village.

017

/Without Frontiers/

WORK GAMES

This is to certify that

...........CEDRIC PRICE...........

the above named participant has endured and survived both natural and unnatural behaviours of the seminar participants & conditions due to such high qualities: Wittiness, Humour, Tolerance, Resistance, Rigour, Discipline.... Since the seminar has sharpened his physical, physiological and psychological qualities and provided him with a new food-alcohol-sleep balance, we truly recomend the participant for any seminar of this kind!

Participants:

SECOND INTERNATIONAL SYMPOSIUM FOR THEORY AND DESIGN IN THE THIRD MACHINE AGE, GROZNJAN AUGUST 17-31 1990

This page:
017. sketch section of halo with indication of function and scale.
018. certificate of attendance.
Opposite:
019. sketch proposals of halo with supporting structure around hilltown site.

018

019

213
MARSHAM ST

A competition entry exploring possible
new uses for a site occupied by three
disused office blocks, formerly occupied
by the Department for the Environment
on Marsham Street, Westminster.
Having visited the buildings on a previous
occasion Price was aware of two
gasometers housed inside blocks.

Coinciding with an increased personal
interest in lidos and the manufacture of
swimming pools ("I was thinking about
them at the time"), he proposes to
demolish the blocks entirely, leaving the
concrete casing of the gasometers intact
and transforming these drums into
two swimming pools; one heated and
one non-heated.

A new elevated plaza/park level
surrounds the pools at first floor level
with the addition of raked seating and
new tree planting, described as a large
flowerbox for shadow and smell.
The shadowed undercroft beneath
the bathing park provides space for a
farmer's market.

Ref: "Marsham Street revisited", BD,
7-14 August 1992.

Changing the density of an area by changing the use —
it's just growing vegetables and having a swim!

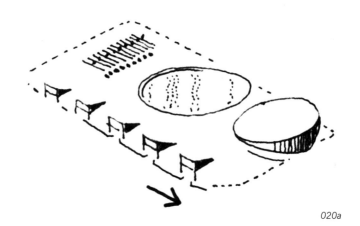

020a

020b

This page:
020a, b. sketch view of pools and seating
on upper level.
Opposite:
021. sketch views of various areas on top
of and underneath the structure: 2 pools,
farmer's market, flower box.
022. plan of roof level.

021

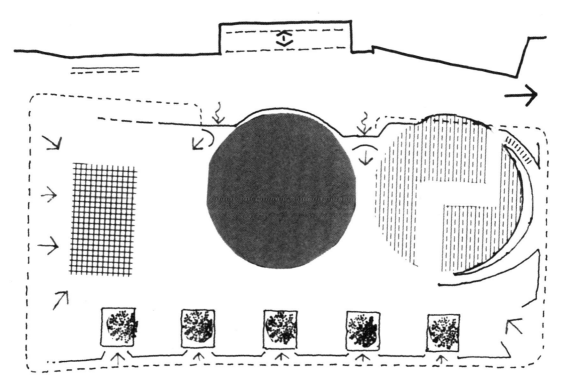

022

196
DUCKLANDS

Hamburg, in common with other major inland ports, has a redundant centre city dockland looking for a new use. At the invitation of the city authority CPA made this proposal: to establish a large nature reserve for migratory waterfowl in a zone where similar reserves are under threat from new industries at the mouth of the Elbe.

The plan includes a series of routes and walkways which connect the "new city foci" *(see sketches: 024 on this page)*, i.e. a bird reserve, with the Old Town by means of light-weight footbridges utilising existing openings and by demolishing areas to make new routes. The mud-mobile *(see sketch collage: 023 on this page)* is one such footbridge; partially submerged in liquid sands, it is a self-powered floating walkway, capable of realignment and self-levelling. It is designed to allow the birds some space and non-disturbance.

A good operational reason for locating the reserve here was that having left Slimbridge on the Severn Estuary, Hamburg is the last stop for birds flying north to Russia, and therefore a good stop off for a hearty meal. Peter Scott, founder of Slimbridge (and Price's friend from the time of working on the AVIARY at London Zoo), had informed the practice about types of birds that would be likely to occupy the reserve at particular times of year and their preferred vegetation. The Institute of Ship Building in Hamburg also helped with information on the behaviour of the migratory population, as they make it their business to know about all aspects of the waterways.

Growing from the existing sand bed, the multi-coloured flowering feed, together with its varied consumers (birds), provide a 'city lung' displaying growth and change. However, the real purpose is to employ short-term, easily established activities, enabling politically, guilt-free long-term strategic thinking by others.

Ref. BD, 11 January, 1991.
Ref. "Cedric Price: Welcoming Water – The City's Lung, an exhibition at the Building Centre, London, 22 November – 22 December '94", review by John Lyall in AA Files no. 29.

023

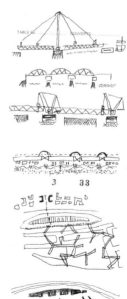

024

Opposite left hand column:
025. Hamburg docklands – areas marked in red proposed for demolition.
026. diagrammatic plan of areas of dockland to be excavated.
027. plan related to assumed reactions of its users/occupiers on completion.

Opposite right hand column:
028. a hint of things to come.
029. diagram of planting types.
030. see note on sketch.

025

A hint of things to come?

028

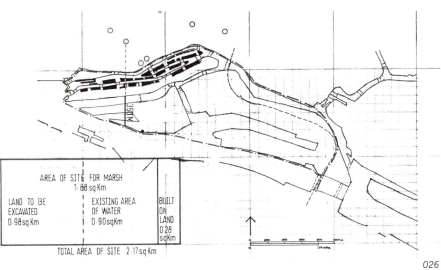

AREA OF SITE FOR MARSH
1·88 sq Km

LAND TO BE
EXCAVATED
0·98 sq Km

EXISTING AREA
OF WATER
0·90 sq Km

BUILT
ON
LAND
0·28
sq Km

TOTAL AREA OF SITE 2·17 sq Km

026

PFLANZEN – DUCK LAND

	MONAT													HÖHE (M)
		1	2	3	4	5	6	7	8	9	10	11	12	
F A R B E			K M	K M	K M	K M	K	K						.15-9
					L	L	L M	L M	L M	M				.30-1
								L	L	L				.30-4
							K M	K M	K M	K M	K			.10-2
			L	L		K M	K M							.10-1
			K M	K M										1-5

TERRAIN: K   SÜMPFE UND MOORE
L   FEUCHTE WIESEN
M   WASSER UND UFER

HOT STUFF
PRESIDENT
CLUB

DUCK LAND

029

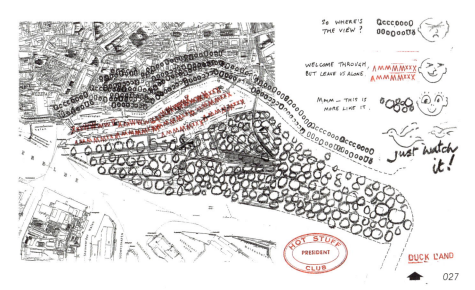

So WHERE'S
THE VIEW ?   Qcccooo0
0oooooUs

WELCOME THROUGH,
BUT LEAVE US ALONE.   AMMMMMXXX
AMMMMMXXX

Mmm — THIS IS
MORE LIKE IT.   o o

just watch
it!

HOT STUFF
PRESIDENT
CLUB

DUCK L'AND

027

The cylical
nature of construction/
architecture / planning
turned into a CLOSED system contained and
constituted in initial design decisions
e.g. Choosing a site and / or Country.

EXISTING
FINITE   TRANSFORM

GROWTH

030

ROBIN MIDDLETON

—

*Robin Middleton, Professor, is an architectural historian. The focus of his studies has been French and English architecture of the eighteenth and nineteenth centuries. He was technical editor of **Architectural Design** from 1964 to 1972, head of general studies at the Architectural Association, London, and librarian and lecturer in the Faculty of Architecture and Art History at Cambridge University from 1972 to 1987. He joined the Columbia University faculty in New York in 1987.*

To Earth.

Within living memory – within my living memory, at least – John Summerson[1], that most sensitive of critics, listed the essentials of architecture as mass, rythmn, texture and outline, in common with music. Cedric Price might have enjoyed Summerson's lectures as a student at the Architectural Association in the 1950s, his diploma project of 1958, "A building of spirit", for the redevelopment of Oldham civic centre shows that he was as much stirred as anyone else at the time by Le Corbusier's formal interventions at Maison Jaoul[2], but thereafter he wanted nothing more of that sort. The architecture he was to explore was to have an altogether different end. The forms of architecture and their pleasing relationships became irrelevant. Instead, an architecture was to be devised that would allow individuals to discover themselves. Even Buckminster Fuller, who was equally mindless of the established conventions of architecture, and by whom Cedric Price was wonderfully stimulated, had less an eye to the finding and expansion of the inner self; Fuller was concerned rather with a physical support system for all individuals, as efficiently contrived that may be. Price had more complex aims. These were sustained at first by a reduction of architecture to the elements of structure, the outcome of which was the AVIARY at London Zoo, which he began to design with Lord Snowdon and engineer, Frank Newby in 1961.

More important by far though were his social concerns, at first undirected, but given marvellous focus in 1962 when he met Joan Littlewood who loathed everything about the complacent, well behaved middle classes. Her Theatre Workshop, at Stratford, in the East End of London, had been established as a bastion of defiance. The theatre, she explained in Joan's Book[3], she had long believed, should provide "space, light and shelter, a place that would change with the seasons,

where all knowledge would be available and new discovery made clear. It was place to play and learn and do what you will. I could not define it philosophically, but its purpose was very clear to me." Price was galvanized. She left soon for Africa, but he took up her dream and when she returned in the following year he showed her the first sketches of what was to become the FUN PALACE. The saga of evolving that giant machine – Frank Newby again, and the "romantic cybernetician", Gordon Pask to hand – is well documented[4]. The undermining and ultimate destruction of the project by the bureaucrats of the Greater London Council,in 1966,is less well known. The FUN PALACE nonetheless served to mark out Cedric Price's territory unequivocally. He could identify himself clearly by then as an "anti-architect". Already he had evolved a project of an even larger scale, and of wilder brilliance, for transforming the derelict infrastructures and the destroyed communities of the North Staffordshire potteries area[5] – destroyed by the Clean Air Act of 1956 – into a realm of higher education, mostly on railroad tracks, but further activated by new computer technologies. No one, as might be imagined, thought seriously to implement so rational a proposal. Ed Berman's INTER-ACTION (later Inter-change) Centre in Kentish Town, London was built in the early 1970s; an assemblage of steel columns and lattice trusses filled with Portakabins, designed on the condition that it had a 20-year life span and accompanied by a manual detailing how the building should be dismantled. Having served as an extraordinarily active focus for the community it is ironic that in 1999 English Heritage and the Twentieth Century Society sought to list the building. To Price's relief the request was thrown out and the building demolished.

Cedric Price's early visionary projects are large and elaborate machines that operate with the first fumblings of

new technologies. Norbert Wiener was already dead when his *Cybernetics, or the control and communication in the animal and the machine*[6] became a cult book amongst architects of radical intent in the late 1960s. Even the promises he held out for the future were soon overtaken by the real advances in information exchange and communication that were available, almost universally, within a few decades. The nature and extent of that change were not foreseen. Soon one could do a lot more of the things that Cedric Price aimed to encourage with a lot less infrastructure, and much handier equipment. A realization of the pattern of change is at once apparent in all his subsequent work; it has become more responsive to the whole environment and more humane, even, than before. The great mechanical features remain, towers are in evidence everywhere, as markers or as supports for equipment. The Thing at the SOUTH BANK is of Leonardo esque enormity and complexity, with up and down spirals and a crown of myriad devices for transmitting, receiving and interacting. Despite all such sophisticated means of communication (see JAPNET's "intelligent plaza" intended for a computerized community without propinquity) the physical links are emphasized as never before. HAVEN, STRATTON, SOUTH BANK and MAGNET are all about links, with railways, motorways, riverways and walkways reinforced wherever possible by a bridge. Price is obsessed with bridges; put down a bridge anywhere, he believes, and someone will establish a need to cross it.

Man-made features are only a part of the new equation. The land and the elements are now being taken aboard. There can be little doubt that Price delighted in the bleakness of the potteries' landscape, but there was no hint in the 1960s that he sought to nurture it. In the more recent proposals landscapes have become features of vital import, most obviously in the proposal to dredge and restore the Channelsea River in MILLS. Sketches show a site peppered with sentinel towers but the bogs and wild growth are retained and enhanced. Notes on the planting of trees and shrubs, ground cover and flowers accompany a great many of the proposals. In SERRE II an exhibition hall is also a giant greenhouse, suspended over water, a "jardin d'eau secret".

Water is another essential feature of the enlarged vision; water moving or still, water as means of transport or as a support system for houseboats. The picturesque was once an anathema, expressly forbidden (it is safe to say that Price had the blurbs of the *Architectural Review* in mind), but now he quotes Wordsworth when exploring the harmony of wind and wave to be sought for a Japanese beach (SURF '90). Itemizing the requirements for a business park near Oslo (SKI), he details the way in which the landscape must be tended to reflect the lights and effects of seasonal changes – "the magic of the site". He states that the ponds and waterways must be left as they are, untrimmed and untidy at the edges. Uvedale Price (no relation) could ask for no more.

The poetic force of the new vision is most in evidence in two extraordinary, undreamed proposals – DUCKLANDS, a plan to turn a large area of disused dockland into a marsh for migrating birds close to the centre of the old town of Hamburg, and IFPRI, the entry for the Canadian Centre for Architecture competition to turn the gash of disused railway tracks behind the old Pennsylvania Railway Station in Manhattan into a vast promenade, an inlet for viewing the city and the Hudson River, a field for experiencing the weather, the winds and the mists, brought in by great stainless steel vanes. A place to breathe. Here the weeds are to be cleared, the hard edge of the city retained.

The imaginative breadth of these two designs has no equal in contemporary architecture. But sheer scale and size are not required to set Price to work. The conversion of a pigsty into a house (GATARD) can set him thinking to enhancing effect, carefully

calculating the initial degree of change required to prompt a response from his client, adapting thus gradually over time.

Rem Koolhaas is reported to have described Cedric Price as a prince who would be a frog; one cannot be altogether sure what he thereby intends, perhaps simply that Price resists success – his drawings are diagrammatic in the extreme, his texts rebarbative, his directives often off-putting; one has to work very hard indeed, not only with the rational mind but with the full force of the imagination to understand the marvellous range of possibilities he offers at any one time. Perhaps Koolhaas seeks to imply that, by putting the fairy tale into reverse, Price is determined to hold the essential, underlying nature of the art with which he deals. I would accept that, but would add that if Price is a prince he is one who has not yet been crowned, neither by his public nor by his private clients, least of all by the profession whose thinking he has done so much to stimulate[7].

ROBERTSON WARD JR

—

Robertson Ward Jr, FAIA, architect, technology researcher, research director, systems' designer, product developer, inventor, maverick explorer... during the 1950s worked in the offices of Konrad Wachsmann, Chicago, Breuer/Nervi, Paris and SOM, Tokyo & Chicago and was Head of Design Technical Research, US Air Force Academy. Between 1960-2002 key projects have included the California S.C.S.D Schools Project, major design commissions for schools of science, the visual and performing arts, director of Renewable Energy projects and the director of nationally funded research grants on the economic functional value of office environments and health care facilities. Robertson Ward Jr has been a Research-Affiliate at M.I.T since 1985.

Cedric Price: Projects '84-'02.

Cedric Price has continued his extraordinary principled pursuit of the **Dynamics of Time** in optimizing actions in the built environment. Areas of his concern and interests have been:

Information in TIME:

Scope: Always concerned with the larger inter-relationships of **resources**, **social needs**, and **allocation policy** and how these change in time.

Process: analysis and synthesis, decisions: How information flows in a ny environmental decision process. How the form and content of information change in the time line of information needs. Early information must be: **succinct**, **relevant**, **minimal**.
What information can describe potential change and value choice? The criticality of variables such as "doubt" and "delight".
Project examples: 1 STRATTON – Diagram: "The Logic of Operation Approximation", an imaging of the effects of different process choices on the result in time. 2 STRATTON – Diagram: "The Logic of Operation Approximation", an imaging of the effects – Diagram: an imaging of the cycling stages of a process encompassing the full life of use, response, and recycle, the identification of discreet intervals.

Communication: A critical element in Price's priorities has always been a recognition of the value of **clarity** and **economy** in both the verbal and graphic images in the necessary presentation of critical information. He has long been a master in achieving an effective short hand of relevant graphics, culled to a minimum effective expression and thereby telegraphing that essence of the content most directly. Every presentation that Price has ever made exhibits this highly refined distillation of the message (some might call it "naïve" who do not recognize its extreme sophistication in the selective design of these critical communication elements – I bless it as good Zen). *Project examples: Choose any project, it is in all Price's work.*
See **MAGNET**, **APPEX**, **MILLS**, *etc. etc.!*

Location in TIME:

Movement: The aspect of geometry and time which develops as a function of **scale** and **mode**. Regional flow and transportation networks; flow at city scale, down to flow in building spatial relationships, flow of people, flow of telecommunication, degrees and strategies of separation, user types, and use intensities and consequent option of routes and network geometries and interactions. Price emphasizes, consistent with his focus on the extended time of various futures, the necessity to predict changes in mode and anticipate the nature of movement systems evolution.
Project Examples: MAGNET exemplifies an anticipatory approach of purposely possible short-term physical bridging mechanisms, flexible and mobile, to create immediate and changeable solutions to inevitable new network demands. The nature of this approach is again a minimum means for maximum effectiveness with inherent adaptability for multiple future configurations.
***STRATTON** and **HAVEN** demonstrate Price's understanding of how multiple modes and separation geometries and concepts of "overloading" and creation of "new lands" and "new waters" can provide new elements of new solutions.*

Function in TIME:

Change: The dynamics of changing functional demands in extended time assigns extraordinary value to the anticipatory performances of flexibility, adaptability, convertability, permutability, interchangeability. Studies of the economic value of these functions as a part of the total functional value of a facility's long-term performance show that they far outweigh the 6% average of physical capital costs. Consequently these functions of future changeability, as Price time and again has emphasized, should receive prime consideration in any proposals for future environmental actions.

To achieve these characteristics in movement systems and built environment and building systems requires rigorous analysis of the particular modes of change which may be anticipated. Determination of the future value of significant modes can begin to identify the minimum set of modes that will achieve adequate future choices. Infinite flexibility is a delusion, inapplicable flexibility is exorbitant, acheiving an adequate flexibility can generate great economic and social value. Price's work has consistently demonstrated his keen awareness of the value of this quest. *Project Examples: again MAGNET provides an outstanding exemplar. Selected elements, developed to satisfy significant modes of performance but able to be reconfigured for a range of anticipated applications because of their inherent provision of the functions of transportability and permutability, supply a continuing solution to a dynamic future in forms, which having been generated by the inherent validity of their design process and may well create a new benchmark of urban expression.*

In contrast, these characteristics in **information systems** have long since been the basis for much of their information effectiveness. Not surprisingly the terminology of microprocessor design is replete with the vocabulary of rationalized building systems: "architecture", "modularity", "orthogonality", "replaceability", "interchangeability", etc. and with the principle that the functional performance of the whole complex is another level above that of the purely physical state of the components.

Participants in TIME:

Price recognizes as an inextricable part of **each movement flow:** the fundamental aspects of the **perceptions**, the **observations**, the **sensory experiences**, the **responses** of the **participants**, both as **individuals** and as various **social groups**. **Information** on how these reactions **change in time**, their **diversity in time**, the **modulations** or **minor variations of seasonality**, **of intensity of flow** contribute to the consequent **pleasure**, **delight**, **learning**, **sense** of **security**, **safety**, **sanctuary**, **friendliness**, **doubt**, or **frustration**, that are **critical components** in the design process **of these futures**.

A new building by Frank Gehry is now going up at the Massachusetts Institute of Technology (M.I.T.) The fixed geometry of its wilful playfulness belies the assertions of "flexibility". These very specific, 3-dimensional "architectural" fixities, particularly in the central village "mixing spaces", may limit and debilitate, rather than enhance their intended function of providing future choices, adaptability, and change of spatial use as a stimulus to a more interactive exchange.

This building will replace and professes to update the legendary "Building 20", called the "Magical Incubator", a "temporary" building built as a research centre for the "Rad Lab" microwave-radar-developer innovators in the early '40s of World War II, a "shabby", simple 30 storey "shack", a scientific "hot house" for 60 years. A building that fostered atomic clocks, Doc Edgerton's superflash bomb run strobes, his underwater cameras, Naom Chomsky's linguistic explorations, Gerry Levin's physiological breakthroughs, James Worden's solar vehicles: a building beloved by all for its acceptance of change, a "rat's nest" of continual improvizations by the innovator occupants. A minimal, adaptable, adequate shell offering the maximum of personal and group choice. The future comparison of the new M.I.T. Gehry building to the "Building 20" it replaces will be revealing.

The essence of the performance of the famed "Building 20" reflects in a modest way a few of the principles consistently pursued by Cedric Price from his earliest work. His aspirations and conceptions of responsive and reactive solutions, of problems from modest scale to multiple levels of complexity and larger regional and social scale, have always offered a clarity of conception, process and presentation, with a stringent, yet enhancing economy of means throughout. Creation of these most significant proposals from the landmark impact of the FUN PALACE to the array of these more recent works has been an enormous contribution of clarity to all those striving toward a more humane and effective built environment.

2 – BRIDGES FOR ALL

RIVERSIDE | RIVERSPAN | RIVER, ESTUARY, OCEAN
C.F. INVISIBLE SANDWICHES

VARIATION OF SET DOWN –
PICK UP

159 SOUTH BANK | 198 STRATTON | 214 HAVEN

TRANSPORT – PLEASURE
FREE WILL TIME – EXISTS | FREE WILL TIME LINKED
WITH LEARNING – NEW | PUBLIC PLEASURE,
PRIVATE/RESIDENT CONVENIENCE

AVOIDANCE OF OLD LONDON BRIDGE ETHIC –
USE OF BRIDGE AS CONTINUOUS FEED – NOT MERELY 'TO GET ACROSS'

OLD LAMPS
ELECTRIFICATION | EVERY LAMP
NEW OIL | NEW LAMPS
OLD OIL

TIME
TIMING | LOCAL
CONVENIENCE | WATER
SETTLEMENT
SITING

TIDAL – RIVER – SEA

TOWN – CITY
COASTAL – CITY
RIVER – CITY
NATIONAL – CITY

RESOURCES
CONTROL
BARRIERS
ENCLOSURE
DEFENCE
IDENTITY
FLOW
CONVENIENCE OF MOVEMENT

2–

BRIDGES
FOR
ALL

214
HAVEN

The proposal is for a new ocean research dock to be established with new city access and communication to accommodate a phased increase in tourism. Mini-magnets (bridges, boardwalk, slope – see MAGNET) make connections between the dockyards, shopping mall and internal streets.

Bremerhaven recognizes the need to increase both tourism and advanced scientific/oceanographic industries to replace declining ship-building and fishing. Assets of the site include the presence of a high quality labour force, several institutes of research and higher education and the proximity of unique facilities in the mass handling of containerised goods, tourists and fish.

"Bridges have had a hard time recently ...it was therefore with some relief that I viewed the Poole Harbour Competition... sited on a lovely and delicate slice of one of the finest and largest harbours in the land. Some entries were over-structured but most had the scale right. However, one aspect that appears to be ignored or underexploited is the element of the design which caters for the public realm. This is often ignored in the new built interventions in an age where the Prime Minister denies the existence of society and cheapens the very word by referring to social housing. In the case of the Poole bridge, over and above its utility and visual delight, and not least because of the use of public monies, it is behoven to serve its unchartered public... remember the Bridge of Sighs."

Periscope, BD, 17 January 1997.

This page:
031. aerial photograph of Bremerhaven dockyard.
Opposite:
032. plan of dockyard site with new routes and bridges marked in red.
033. journey times.
034. sketch of new beach meeting water (marine scope).

It is suggested that both the 21st century citizen and tourist will be interested in a fuller understanding of the marvels of the present and the challenge of the future than in nostalgia and the mysteries of the past.

Three new bridges provide improved public access, observation, convenience and safety. Each has a particular usefulness related to its siting.

a) The Boardwalk – acts as a high level threshold to the marine slope and partial shelter to mobile facilities below.

b) The Marine Slope – self-ventilated stepped concrete structure doubling the area of inclined seaside available to all.

c) The New Dock – a purpose-built calibrated dock to accommodate test rigs, traveling cranage and robotic locators for a variety of marine technological investigations initiated by local and national research institutes, universities and industry.

Demolition of the majority of existing buildings provides space for laboratory workshops and temporary structures enabling specialized trade fairs.

A range of tourist amenities are housed inside wheeled units capable of re-locating when not in use and storage beneath the bridges. A power supply is to be taken from the columns of the boardwalk (ref. WESTAL).

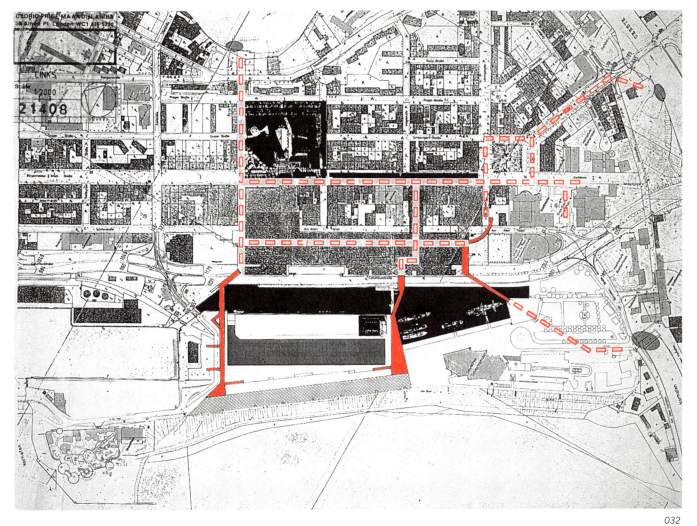

032

HAVEN

214/M/002

JOURNEY TIMES (II)

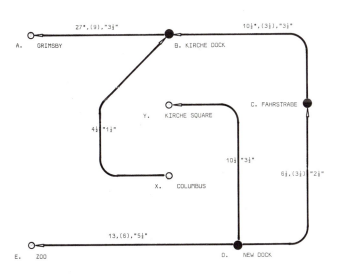

A. GRIMSBY   27*,(9),"3½"   B. KIRCHE DOCK   10½*,(3½),"3½"

Y. KIRCHE SQUARE   C. FAHRSTRABE

4½ "1½"   10½ "3½"   6½,(3½) "2½"

X. COLUMBUS

E. ZOO   13,(6),"5½"   D. NEW DOCK

KEY   XX: MOST DIRECT WALKING TIME (minutes) @ 5km/h
       XX*:   RIVERSIDE WALKING TIME   (minutes) @ 5km/h
      (XX):   RIVERBUS JOURNEY TIME   (minutes) @15km/h
     "XX":   MOST DIRECT CYCLING TIME (minutes) @15km/h

033

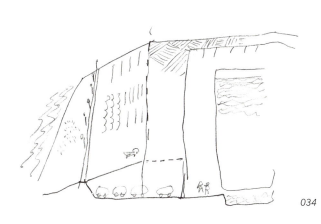

034

THE NEXT GENERATION
OF CITIZENS OF
BREMERHAVEN
DO NOT ALL WANT TO BE
MUSEUM ATTENDANTS
OR SHOE SALEMEN
HOWEVER ADMIRAL SUCH
JOBS MAY BE.

198
STRATTON

A cross-Rhine international road link, Strasbourg–Kehl, together with phased new development of an industrial and dockland zone. A new TGV station and motorway are included in the proposed educational, industrial and community plan development to be administered by a new Joint Cities authority. The new road and rail facility enables a variety of uses below, while the motorway itself is incorporated within larger activity volumes. Long-term redevelopment of industrial polluted land creates new demolition and horticultural industries.

"No-one should be interested in building bridges – they should be interested in how to get to the other side."

Cedric Price, Pegasus, 1972.

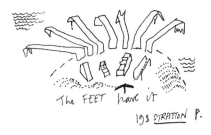

The FEET have it

198 STRATTON P.

Opposite:

35. the logic of operational approximation diagram.

Page 038:

036a, b, c, d. sketches of possible bridges between road, rail and water.

037. sketch of railway station.

038. plan of area.

Page 039:

039. sketch section showing relation of road to rail and undergound links.

040. plan of Strasbourg site with marks in red indicating concentrations of activity to be linked.

041. plan with key to proposed areas and types of activity to be developed.

HISTORY

In the past, CITIES were located where barriers could be crossed and defensive positions held. Later, CITIES became the junction of trade routes by both land and water and meeting places for all in the region. Local resources of materials and energy were exploited and industries established. Markets were generated and goods exchanged and stored. Successive forms of physical communication by road, rail and water were later supplemented by invisible forms such as telephone, radio, television and computer networks. Due to their invisible network of communications and exchange the reasons for physical communication and congregation became more particularised. Learning, leisure and tourism became major industries. The more conventional industries found the rigid nature of the existing cities increasingly restrictive. Citizens were able to congregate through choice rather than necessity. Regional activities including agriculture extended their networks of exchange and wealth creation beyond particular foci, such as markets and wholesale warehouses. Particular communities together with their chosen facilities fragmented and reformed in patterns and forms unrelated to existing physical forms and plans. The visual delights of the great old city are numerous and easily accessible. The qualities of the community, as detailed by Erasmus, are less easy to discern but even more valuable.

SITE

The unique quality of the site is invisible. It is the international border that, for the first time, must unite rather than divide this whole area and the region beyond. The successor to the city/town includes massive means of transportation in a variety of forms and speeds, above, at and below ground level. This super-zone is (at the time of writing this report)an ideal condition to generate a new form of 21st century urban centrality. The process and products resulting from this project should provide an invaluable living prototype for future European Development.

A role of both architecture and planning is both to facilitate cultural change and enable cultural excellence.

Existing cities, centuries old, must be viewed in many respects as "natural hazards" with good and bad qualities like a forest or a swamp.

The "city" of the future requires the fourth dimension, time, as an integral part of its formation, operation and capacity to change.

The justification for the continuing of existing cities must be on terms of that which it enables in the future.

PROPOSALS

In these proposals, the movement patterns, new and established, are the Form Givers.

There is a vast amount of stored information in the area, particularly within the Universities. Existing and the new activities proposed should be harnessed by means of the latest educational technologies to become a community resource available to all. These proposals envisage the rapid creation of a "European classroom" for all ages.

These proposals require methods of major demolition, reinstatement and the installation of major sub-service surfaces. Such installation will involve the latest and in some cases, experimental, methods, techniques and processes. In so doing a series of new industries are established within the project area, eg. an integrated demolition and material recycling mobile factory large area enabling controlled chemical, explosive and implosion techniques, centralised impact crushing, on-site bulk movement, rubble screening and recycling and material sorting and batching for new construction. This installation of a vast 'living' continuous demonstration for technology associated with the creation and maintenance of landscape is unique in the European Community. In addition to its economic, technological and educational value, applied technologies are to include: artifical intelligence, robotics, information technology, materials, mechnisation, hydroponics. Probably the most important new industry is that which will result from the interaction between high technology for agriculture and horticulture and environmental amenity development.

The proposals are to be phased over three time periods: 0-2 years, 2-6 years, and 0-6+ years. The richness is in the fragmentation of the parts but only remains rich if all those parts are accessible at the same time, i.e. have equal status. The phasing of the plan, as to the accessibility and usefulness of the new order, is made possible by the presence of the bridge.

THE HALO - to be established over the years, a 1000 metre diameter ring of recognition and pride. To be delineated in a variety of forms and media and seen as a unique symbol of this new pan-European venture, taking its place together with the spire of Notre Dame Cathedral, the majesty of the Rhine and the beauty of the surrounding countryside.

A synergy of movement and location replaces boundries and territory.

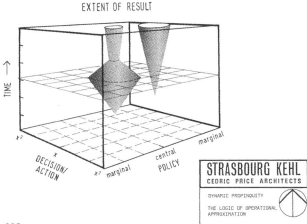

or... Ships that pass in the night...

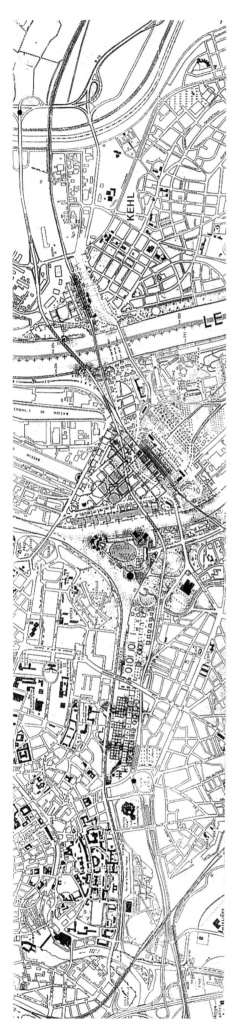

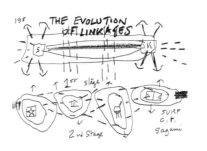

036a

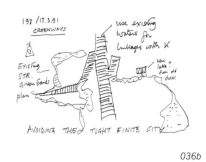

036b

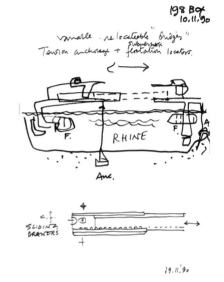

TGV
+ exhibit city

036c

198 BO
10.11.90

variable · relocateable "bridges"
Tension anchorage + flotation locators.

RHINE

c.f.
SLIDING
DRAWERS

19.11.90

036d

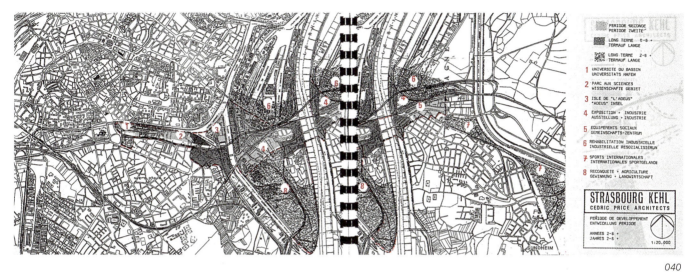

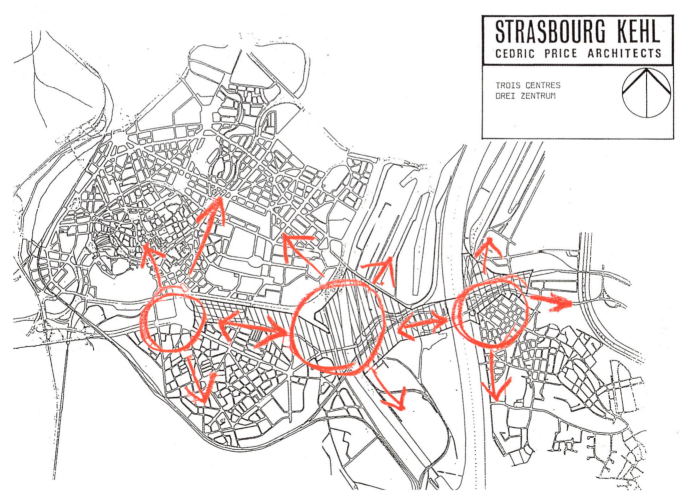

STRASBOURG KEHL
CEDRIC PRICE ARCHITECTS

TROIS CENTRES
DREI ZENTRUM

159
SOUTH BANK

In 1983 Tony Banks MP, then chairman of the Arts & Recreation Committee of the Greater London Council, initiated the commissioning of CPA to investigate methods whereby the South Bank, then largely owned by the GLC, could be enhanced. Price's first impression of the site: "It's like a de Chirico painting".

"A city should be sufficiently old, rich, and well-serviced to be able to accommodate a vast range of disparate, peculiar, incomparable objects, space, activities and people. The resultant mix, to be both convivial and convenient, is achieved through constant change in community appetites and individual mores – and not through a Band-aid of architectural ingenuity trying to be all things to all men..."

Price Probes, BD, 16 September 1994.

Ref: "Urban Initiative", BD, 23 September 1998
Ref: Ian Latham, "South Bank Saviour?", BD, 3 February 1984.

Page 042:
042. photocopy collage view of the South Bank taken from artist, Felix Topolsky's top-floor apartment on the Embankment.
Page 043:
*043. spread of plan for South Bank site with proposals as presented in **Building Design**, 23 September 1988.*
Page 044:
044a, b. sketches of new public space spanning the River Thames. "Too big to be called a bridge"
045. sketch section showing supporting framework throughout the site.
046a, b, c. location and aspects of The Thing.
Page 045:
047. working sketch of big wheel.
048. "superimposition of self-supporting framework".
049a, b. sketches of triangular towers.

This is about the avoidance of the Old London Bridge ethic and preconceptions of the old riverside. The proposals are necessarily concerned with establishing a framework: from the installation of a new system of administration to the ordering of existing spaces and accentuating the impact of the elements upon its surfaces. Any new structure is ambiguous in use and for the most part is 'supportive', i.e. for refreshment, relaxation or information. The site area covers 270 acres, the equivalent of Soho and Covent Garden put together, half water and half land. Most importantly, the South Bank is a National, Metropolitan and Communal amenity.

The place is at present a mess - a mixture of inward looking activities that ignore the space between them ...the largest single area, the river, is ignored. It must be made available for massive human individual and collective endeavour, skill, delight and imagination... more than a city lung.

The South Bank is still associated with that lovely limited-life celebration of 1951, the Festival of Britain. However, the Festival took place throughout the United Kingdom – the South Bank was merely the most architecturally noteworthy manifestation. A largely derelict site bordered by a declining thoroughfare, the Thames, its selection for an experiment bears similarities with Docklands and King's Cross Goods Yard, with one important difference; the former was a manifestation of national pride, the latter opportunities for private greed.

But the festival was 37 years ago, when private telephones and televisions were scarce, credit cards unknown, men covered their heads, and I first visited London.

To transfer concern into action in any area of a late 20th century metropolis, one should have little time for nostalgia. To look at such an area is to investigate:

Regions of responsibility
Fields of usefulness
Zones of effect
Volumes of opportunity

But uppermost is the need to realise that no urban space is operationally finite, that no plan has a single scale and that no artifacts are timeless. City structures and systems as found are the natural hazards of the future. All cities last too long, but thankfully, all cities eventually fall. The architect in accepting the latter should ameliorate the former. Demolition must not merely be a palliative, as at Ronan Point (ref.), but be a cause of celebration of the future. Change is inevitable but the change of choice is heady stuff.

No city that lives is static. Calculated uncertainty and conscious incompleteness combine with benign fragmentation to form the three Canons of the Design.

PROPOSALS

By concreting over a section of the River Thames to create a public space much bigger than Trafalgar Square (too big to be called a bridge) and therefore being of another dimension, it can no longer be called the North or South Bank. The establishment of large uncommitted areas existing and speculative is essential throughout tired old cities to enable rethink by others. That done, proposals for adding to or taking away from the existing site may commence.

An infrastructure of towers, relocatable, triangular and of steel may pepper parts of the site, not merely the South Bank - indeed they can be river-based and prototypical for general city usage. Providing access links, anchorage and suspension for shelter or screens they are in themselves incomplete, merely providing "space hooks and hurdles". These are to be accompanied by a system of floating pontoon structures and massed, retractable banked public seating connecting and bridging existing structures on the site. Also, a lightweight variable structure or "umbrella" that can be assembled in under 4 hours to provide shelter for between 50,000-100,000 people.

The basement areas of County Hall are denuded by the installation of possibly the world's most palatial underground station to be called the Riverside Rail County Hall Station, with an additional station at the Royal Festival Hall. The railway runs above and below ground and water level providing rapid public access. The length of the line can vary with demand. Putting a concrete boxed tunnel in Thames mud is not too tricky.

The Thing's dimensions were determined by the fact that London is cow-pat bland if viewed from too great a height. Cabins called "globes" are attached to an all steel tower structure. Each globe carries up to 30 people, continuously moving up and down the tower, slowly revolving all the time (one car every one and a half minutes, travel time 4 minutes). Passengers may get out at the top onto open decks, their food having travelled up in a similar cabin and positioned on one of the decks according to the weather and time. The summit is crowned by an indeterminate framework awaiting inevitable electronic growths. The impact of the Thing's base on Waterloo Circus helps to establish a new identity for an existing space.

Ten intermediate floors of The Shell Centre are removed. The subsequent reduction of services and vertical access loading creates two viable office units with a centralized protected observation and exchange "shelf". Elsewhere within the Shell complex, an open ice rink is installed and a market square established. The establishment of linkages within and beyond the considered area is engineered not merely to reduce the "cultural ghetto" quality of the present development, but more importantly to introduce at an early stage real examples of such city linkages that will eventually become appropriate to urban and suburban growth. The footbridge (an axially supported steel suspension structure) linking Trafalgar Square and the Strand with the South Bank, moves above the existing Hungerford Rail Bridge. It combines two-way travelators, a central walkway and observation decks. It is not covered - London requires raincoats.

Other city-wide applications are prototyped in the area, including the painting of concrete gloss cream (whereby all can see that by its necessary upkeep the South Bank is being looked after for them), phased arboreal husbandry (in places to crowd out both people and buildings), the siting of eating and drinking facilities as if fountains and sculpture, the use of lighting as a giant time-teller and the allowance for people to walk over a greenhouse as well as through it.

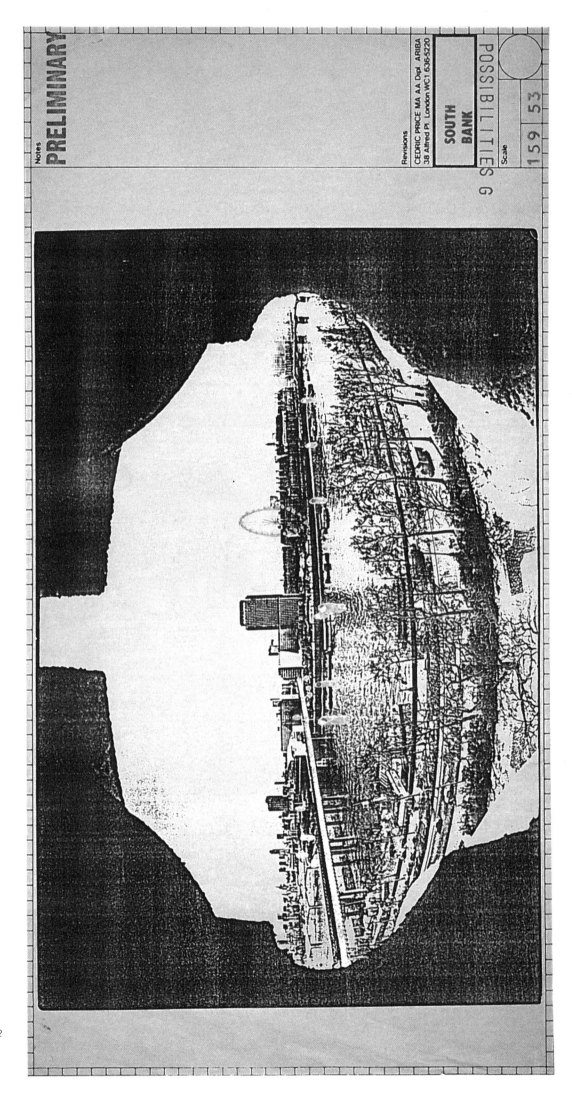

PRELIMINARY

Notes

Revisions

CEDRIC PRICE MA AA Dipl. ARIBA
38 Alfred Pl. London WC1 636-5220

SOUTH
BANK

POSSIBILITIES G

POSSIBILITIES

Scale

159 53

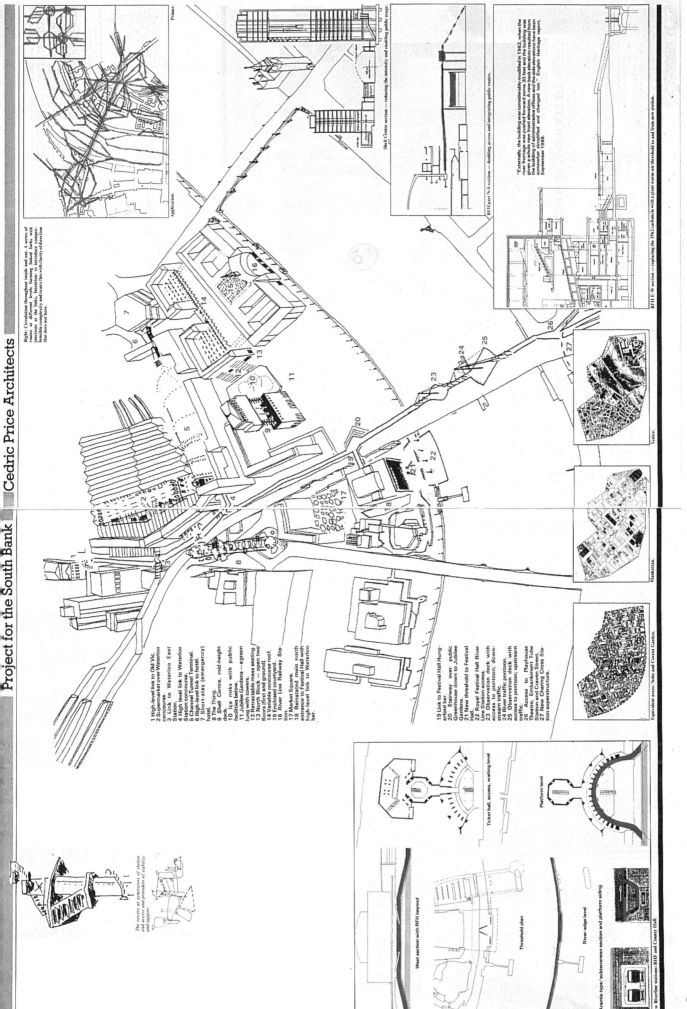

Right: Circulation throughout inside and out. A series of routes at different levels forming linked forks with junctions at intervals to introduce comprehensible complexity and to mix this with clarity of direction that does not bore.

Primer.

Application.

The towers as generators of shelter and access and providers of stability and support.

1 High-level link to Old Vic.
2 Supermarket over Waterloo concourse.
3 Link to Waterloo East Station.
4 High level link to Waterloo Station concourse.
5 Channel Tunnel Terminal.
6 High-level link to hotel.
7 Short-stay (emergency) hotel.
8 The Thing.
9 Shell Centre, mid-height deck.
10 Ice rinks with public facilities below.
11 Jubilee Gardens —a green lung with towers.
12 Retractable mass seating.
13 North Block — open two floors (first and ground).
14 Variable concourse roof.
15 Enclosed courtyard.
16 River Line Railway Station.
17 Market Square.
18 Reinstated main north entrance to Festival Hall with high-level link to Waterloo bar.
19 Link to Festival Hall Hungerford bar.
20 Stairway over public Greenhouse down to Jubilee Gardens.
21 New threshold to Festival Hall.
22 Royal Festival Hall River Line Station access.
23 Observation deck with access to pontoon; downstream traffic.
24 River traffic pontoon.
25 Observation deck with access to pontoon; upstream traffic.
26 Access to Playhouse Theatre, Embankment Tube Station and Craven Street.
27 New Charing Cross Station superstructure.

Equivalent areas: Soho and Covent Garden.

Venice.

Manhattan.

Shell Centre section — reducing the intensity and enabling public usage.

RFH part N-S section — flooding access and integrating public routes.

"Externally, the building was considerably modified in 1962, when the river frontage was pushed forward. A new back elevation resulted from the building of administrative offices and the side elevations have been somewhat simplified and changed too." — English Heritage report, September 1988.

RFH E-W section — replacing the 1962 carbuncle with a giant warm-air threshold to and from new station.

West section with RFH beyond

Threshold plan

River-edge level

Ticket hall, access, waiting level

Platform level

New Riverline station: RFH and County Hall.

Artemis-type/subterranean section and platform siding.

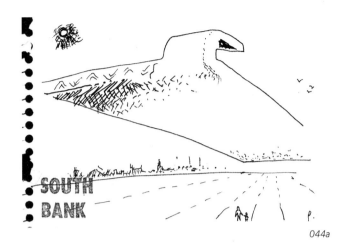

SOUTH
BANK

044a

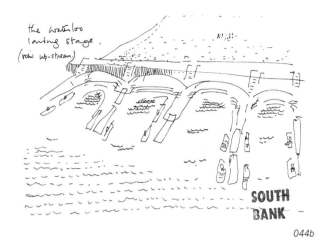

the Waterloo
landing stage.
(view up-stream)

SOUTH
BANK

044b

045

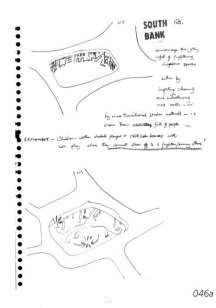

SOUTH
BANK

046a

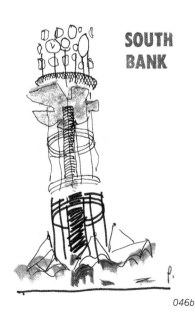

SOUTH
BANK

046b

The Things Base 159. 20 8.
186

The Worm
Our Straw
Hat

SERVICE

'There was an old woman
who...

IN 'n'
OUT
Shelters?

CEDRIC PRICE MA Cantab. ARIBA AA Dipl. ARCHITECT
38 ALFRED PLACE LONDON WC1E 7DP Tel: 01-636

SOUTH
BANK

046c

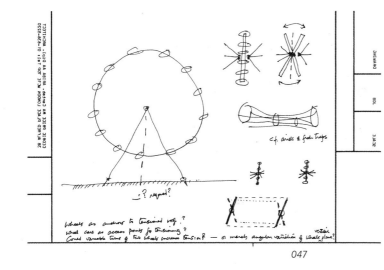

	SCALE	JOB	DRAWING

wheels as anchors to tensioned roof?
wheel cars as access points for tensioning?
Curved variable trim of this wheels increase tension? — or merely angular variation of wheels plane?

c.f. aviers & fish traps

.? repeat?

047

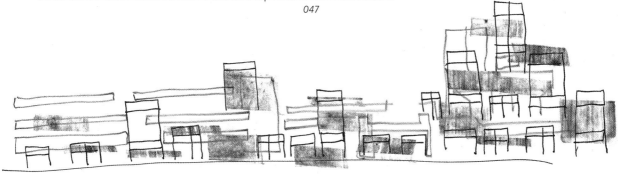

the superimposition of self-supporting frame-works
introducing bridging order vertically & sheltered convenience horizontally

**SOUTH
BANK**

P.

048

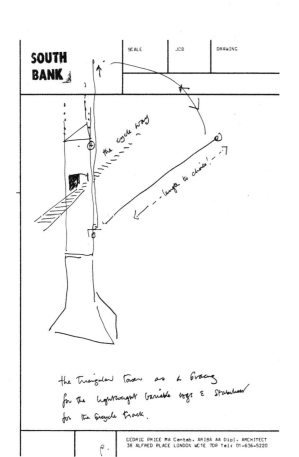

**SOUTH
BANK**

SCALE	JOB	DRAWING

the cycle way

--- length to chain! --7

the Triangular Tower as a bracing
for the lightweight variable roys & stadium
for the bicycle track.

P.

049a

159.

**SOUTH
BANK**

Any future in having
a truncated △ Tower?

TOBLERONE

the unshakeable . an horizontal Tower

049b

JOHN FRAZER

——

John Frazer, Professor, trained at the Architectural Association, taught first at Cambridge University and then the AA in the 1970s and again in the '90s. He was Head of School of Design Research History and Criticism at the University of Ulster in the 1980s, he also ran a systems and design consultancy with his wife Julia (including projects for Cedric Price and Walter Segal) and was founder and chairman of Autographics software. He is currently Swire Chair Professor and Head of School of Design in Hong Kong.

This is a very personal perspective on a concept of universal and future significance. It is personal, both in the sense that it is an unashamedly biased view of both the significance of the project, and the nature of that significance and because the author was personally involved as one of the consultants on GENERATOR and subsequently involved Cedric Price in its educational application at the Architectural Association. GENERATOR is still very much alive and was still developing whilst this chapter was being written.

The Continuing Relevance of GENERATOR – The Archetypal Generator. The fundamental concepts of FUN PALACE, POTTERIES THINKBELT and GENERATOR are models for a future architecture as yet unrealized. These are not so much projects but generic ideas about new ways of making environments responsive to the needs and desires of their users. They represent a fundamental archetype of a new deal for users – or a new menu in Cedric Price's terminology.

Price had introduced concepts of response and change into the FUN PALACE and POTTERIES THINKBELT schemes, and to date FUN PALACE has been regarded as the archetypal Price project possibly due to its monumentalization in the Pompidou Centre (1972-76). FUN PALACE is also loved by architectural historians who can find authority for it (and themselves) by finding precedents such as Jean Prouvé's Maison de Peuple (1939)[1]. Although when Reyner Banham first wrote about FUN PALACE, he talked not in terms of precedent, but by showing how as both a concept and a programme, it had far greater social relevance and conceptual significance than the other contemporary "people's palace" – the then new Crystal Palace Sports Centre[2].

Banham recalled that Price drove the press mad for months by refusing to show drawings of what the FUN PALACE would *look like* and Banham suspected that even Cedric

Price might not know but "…that was not the point. Seven nights of the week it will probably look like nothing on earth from the outside: the kit of service towers, lifting gantries and building components exists solely to produce the kind of interior environments that are necessary and fitting to whatever is going on. What matters is that the various activity-spaces inside the Fun Palace will not be fossilized in a single architectural schema that may be functionally out of date in five years…" The drawings and model that Price did publish show negative images, enigmatically labelled "control", "movement", "response".

The real difficulty with the FUN PALACE was not that no-one knew what it might look like, but that it was never clear how it would be controlled and who would have the fun of controlling all the gantries and moving parts.

However, GENERATOR offers a clear programme of how, and why, change is to be effected and what the variation in resulting environments might be like. GENERATOR comes with a completely worked out strategy for self-organization. It poses the notion of an intelligent building that learns from its own experience. GENERATOR is a field of reconfigurable cubes with supporting cast of sun shades, walkways, hurricane props and a mobile crane. The proposition is fully detailed in both physical and system terms so it could be tested (in an abstract sense) and evaluated (in some sense at least).

"Architecture should have little to do with problem-solving – rather it should create desirable conditions and opportunities hither to thought impossible." Cedric Price[3]

Formlessness: "Forms beget forms whereas ideas barely have any influence on them", Philip Johnston. Architectural history and theory almost invariably serve a history or theory of form rather than ideas. Reyner Banham was one significant exception and Roy Landau was another, but otherwise

the idle critics have so far ignored Price's contribution or marginalized it. Peter Eisenman dismisses the polemics of Reyner Banham, Cedric Price and Archigram as "English revisionist functionalism" seeing their thinking as neo-functionalism with an idealization of technology, yet invested with the same ethical positivism and aesthetic neutrality as the early Modern Movement, but now with moral criteria substituted for those of a more formal nature[4].

Adrian Forty sees FUN PALACE as "formless" and would doubtless apply the same epithet to GENERATOR. He sees it as "formless" because it was a structure with an indeterminate form, capable of endless rearrangement – this, of course, is indeterminacy not formlessness, but Forty is making the point in the context of a tradition embracing Buckminster Fuller and promoted by Reyner Banham whom he believes was hostile to form. "But Banham's hostility to 'form' was connected principally with an enthusiasm for technological innovation: the lesson he drew from the work of Buckminster Fuller in particular was that a purely technical construction might lead to results that would be unrecognisable as architecture"[5]. That is architecture as we know it, or at least thought we knew it before Price made his propositions. Price's work espouses flexibility rather than indeterminacy, driven not by a technological imperative, but a concern for the flexible needs and appetites of the users. I would contend that there is nothing "formless" or even "indeterminate" about his projects. They most certainly have form and it is determinate (at least the enabling structure and systems – and indeed the form itself at any one moment) – determined by the preferences and needs of the users rather than imposed by the formal whim of the architect. Price is free of the formalism of traditional inflexible and overly determined form in architecture.

Roy Landau in *New Directions in British Architecture* sees indeterminacy as being the basis of the *new directions* of his title. "He [Price] has approached indeterminacy as an ideal which can be shown to have a very special appropriateness to a range of architectural questions..." "work... possessing almost no arbitrary formal allegiances...[6]"

In relation to cultural values: "In the Thinkbelt project, the designer stops well short of offering the occupant, say an ash-tray (on the grounds that there is no guarantee that the designer and the occupant have the same cultural values), while at CBS, the designers only allow him one approved by Florence Knoll (since there is no guarantee that the designer and the occupant have the same cultural values).[7]" This is a promising start to a chapter by George Baird *"La Dimension Amoureuse"* meaning in *Architecture* where Baird plays off Price's POTTERIES THINKBELT scheme against Saarinen's CBS building. Baird goes on to argue that they are both wrong! But the initial juxtaposition is startling.

Michael Hays sees Price as having diverted architecture to purely utilitarian ends, toward the regenerative potential of accessible education in the economically depressed English Midlands [POTTERIES THINKBELT]. His commitment is not to architecture but to some value or effect outside of architecture, which architecture is to serve.

The GENERATOR –
The Birth of the Intelligent Building.
Cedric Price is unequivocal in seeing architecture serving the user: "A forest facility for 1-100 users. Architecture is used as an aid to the extension of one's own interests. A series of structures, fittings and components that respond to the appetites that they themselves may generate. A 'menu' of items for individual and group demands of space, control, containment and delight. A place to work, create, think and stare." So starts Price's own description of GENERATOR.

GENERATOR (1976 onwards) proposed a kit of parts which enabled enclosures, gangways, screens and services to be arranged in a clearing in a forest in Florida to fulfil the requirements of the users who were to be the employees of the Gilman Paper Corporation. The forest floor was gridded with foundation pads and a mobile crane was to be permanently on

site to move around parts of the structure to provide endless reconfiguration. A suite of computer programs was developed (1979) to suggest new arrangements of the site in response to changing needs[8]. It was proposed to embed microelectronics into every part of the structure and connect them through the foundation grid so that the whole structure would know where all the parts were. Thus all parts of the structure would co-operate to compute new configurations to meet changing user needs and responses. In the event of the users not suggesting many changes, then the building itself would get "bored" and start suggesting alterations and thus promote a learning cycle by which the building would learn how best to configure itself to meet the users needs and perhaps stimulate new appetites[9].

Price had a regular weekly slot in *Building Design* and in January 1979 he wrote "Just to add to the computer in architecture debate I include this proposal from my consultant on our latest project in which this friendly machine is widely used. 'The site and the elements on it should have a life and intelligence of their own and the program would start to generate unsolicited plans, improvements and modifications in response to users, comments, records of activities, or even by building-in a boredom concept so that the site starts to make proposals about changes of itself if no changes are made.' Now such a proposal can only work if the initial design allows for layouts and structures that can alter and decay and disappear. Mine can..."

The press were quick to pick up on this...

RIBA Journal, June 1980 is headlined "WORLD'S FIRST INTELLIGENT BUILDING" and describes how microprocessor chips will be incorporated into the building fabric and how the different computer programs would organize the site and again latches on to the concept of boredom as the logical conclusion of Price's ideas about interactive buildings over a 20 year period. The article concludes: "The computer program is not merely a passive computer aided design program nor is it just being used to assist with the organisation of the site, but is being used actively to encourage continual change and adaptation to changing requirements." Deyan Sudjic headlined in *Design*, January 1981:

"Birth of the Intelligent Building" and says "Long before he began the project, Price was determined to create environmentswhich could instantly respond to their inhabitants' immediate needs. Labelling a room on a plan has a paralysing effect on the way it's used. Today it appears he's set off on a course that could rid us of those paralysing effects once and for all."

New Scientist, 19 March 1981, talked of "A building that moves in the night". "But to call it a building is an understatement; for, by means of a few instructions from a central computer, the building can change its shape and layout to meet the needs of people inside it".

Although Price generously credited his consultants for adding this idea of intelligence to the building, the idea was actually intrinsic to the building concept. GENERATOR as a proposition was essentially an intelligent building to which the consultants just added the electronics and the software.

Neil Spiller recently revisited this issue in the *Cyber Reader* and reflects my own view: "Important new ideas emerged from the Generator project. These included embedded intelligence and learning from experience during use, the isomorphism of processor configuration and structure, and the question of consciousness... [of intelligent buildings]". Spiller goes on, "This important symbiosis, examined in Price's architectural thesis of 'enabling' and the use of the computer, sets a benchmark against which most contemporary 'intelligent' buildings (and their designers) can be measured."

Computing without computers.
"Technology is the answer – but what was the question?" – So Cedric starts the slide presentation of GENERATOR[10].

Raising questions is one of Price's great strengths, or "The question-ing of indisputable premises" as Roy Landau once put it. The asking of questions is the fundamental driver of a radical studio. As Samantha Hardingham wrote when she asked me to write this chapter, "My first encounter with Cedric and then time spent at the AA was critical in forming my understanding of what architecture could be; presenting architecture in non-aesthetic terms but rather as a system of values, to be questioned.[11]" Cedric Price himself when asked what architects brought to the table replied "Continually questioning the premise. Continually questioning as a process". He went on to say that he "used schools as a greedy alternative to posing my own questions"[12]. Far from greedy, Price is famous for his generosity in giving lectures and participating in critiques, he is equally famous for rarely accepting invitations to teach on a regular basis. But in 1987 he agreed to be a resident critic to my new diploma unit at the Architectural Association. Projects that benefited from his critique included an "Exploratory of space and time" and "An evolutionary". But it was asking questions, particularly about the role of technology, which most challenged the students. Following on in 1989, with encouragement from Price, Alvin Boyarsky, the then Chairman of the Architectural Association, took a very radical step and allowed the unit to embark on a five year experiment using computers in a radically new way and with no projects in the conventional and then understood sense. Price's role was critically that of a questioner.

One of the first thought experiments we posed to the new unit which was to be heavily concerned with computers was about computing without computers – the engagement with technology without the inconvenience. Whilst Price was always one of the first to understand the potential of new technology, he was far too sensible to actually use it. Hence in his office there were notoriously no voice messages (he didn't want to "waste the morning answering yesterday's problems"), no fax (at least not with paper in it), no word processor and no computer drafting. Technology was best as a thought experiment – hence computing without computers.

But Price has no hesitation in consulting cyberneticians and systems experts, and typically appointed Gordon Pask at an early stage to FUN PALACE and went on to collaborate on the Japanese housing scheme (JAPNET) for a competition much later on in 1990. In a remarkable essay entitled "The Architectural Relevance of Cybernetics" (published with extraordinary vision by *Architectural Design* in September 1969) Pask makes a convincing case for the emerging significance of cybernetics to architecture. He establishes that there had arisen a *demand* for system oriented thinking whereas in the past there had been only a more or less esoteric *desire* for it (Gordon's italics).

And he cites FUN PALACE as key example. Actually it was the only example at that time, but Pask ingeniously argues that Gaudi's Parque Guell could be regarded as a cybernetic structure!

In 1990, Price participated in one of a series of introductory exercises called CHOICE with the AA Diploma 11 students. The brief began with a quote from Cedric, "Taking infinite pains with a problem is best left to the computer; making a choice is the human's role"[13]. The brief goes on "This exercise will test your thinking so far by looking at the Generator project. You will be required to hypothesize rules and procedures for organizing the Generator and simulate the results with models. Propose how the computer might be useful or otherwise but try to refrain from using it." "Cedric will introduce the Generator at 11.00am on 8 November." The thinking behind GENERATOR inspired another group of students with its timeless relevance.

GENERATOR – next move.
Inspired by talking again with Price recently in London, and in the midst of writing this chapter I decided to go ahead and build one of the models which we had previously proposed. We built one working model with embedded electronics in 1980[14], and proposed further more elaborate models with higher levels of embedded intelligence as late as 1990. Developments in economically available single chip microprocessors now make it economically viable to construct two new models that will demonstrate aspects of GENERATOR that have so far not been seen. Each cell of the model will have a powerful on board processor, camera to see viewer reaction and display screen to indicate what the cell is "thinking". A robot arm will be integral to the system to move the cells around on a gridded baseboard. There will be no external computer, all the computation about the configuration of the model will be done by the array of the cells. The whole system will be "conscious" at least to the limited extent of being self-conscious of its own configuration and it will be able to learn by viewing spectator reaction (representing the users). GENERATOR still has much to say to those who believe that architecture should serve the users, and a new model might speak to a new generation who might yet realize the future of which Cedric Price has given us a vision.

NEIL SPILLER

—

Neil Spiller is Reader in Architecture and Digital Theory at the University of Buffalo, Texas, U.S.A and a practising architect. He is the Diploma/MArch (Architecture) Course Director and Vice Dean (Academic Affairs) at the Bartlett School of Architecture, University College, London. He is currently writing the definitive history of twentieth century visionary architecture.

Don't forget the undersides.

Currently, architectural vision is at a low ebb. What passes for the contemporary cutting edge is a three-way split between the normative ugliness of the "Super Dutch", the cyber-porn of the blobists and the filthy, rampant capitalism of "Bigness". In these circumstances, it is necessary to be reminded of the work of Cedric Price. "Work" seems totally the wrong word. "Work", often synonymous with "unhappy toil" is not the way to talk about Price or his output. He has a history of producing benevolent architecture. His very definition of the practice is as a discipline consisting of purveyors of fun, humour and humanity. His architecture is neither tinged with techno-libertarian selfishness nor in thrall to the vicissitudes of fickle fashion. His architecture is "cool", not cool-trendy, but self-effacing, enabling, appropriate, expedient and at its best even invisible – the odd organisational tweak of a strategy or system might be enough to save it from institutional stasis. The "work" has a selfless, sparing elegance.

On a good day, the English do have a weird take on architecture found nowhere else in the world, and Price is very English. He is one of architecture's great humanist thinkers – and – let's face it – there aren't many of those wandering about outside the squalid narcissistic scrum of the architectural profession. He is a wonderful teacher, talker and polemicist. What he has to offer real and virtual worlds is fundamental in mitigating tendencies in both realms towards exclusion, disconnectedness, ignorance and a propensity and to look at the object as obstacle.

With the evolution of virtual space and its real world bundle of plastic and chips, the number of ideas that Price has poured forth since the 1960s has become even more important for us to learn. The contemporary city changes at a phenomenal rate, it is in some sense alive. Its traces, vectors and memories as well as its current physical manifestation are all the "sites"

for enabling architectures. The city's evolving spatial fecundity needs to be navigated, connected and choreographed over time. Duration and event are the life-blood of the city; this notion is becoming more and more powerful as the city creates its own trans-geographies, slipping parts of itself fleetingly into other cities. Price has shown us some of the main tactics that architects of the future will doubtless need.

If we consider your or my back garden (or if you are in America, backyard) superimposed over it is a whole massively complex world, an ecology always rearticulating itself. Next-door's back garden is similar but different. Your kitchen is planned differently to your neighbour's and you use the space differently. Different things are important to you and to your neighbour – you may like Monet, he may like the ball-game. People are different and have a demand for a personalised architecture to call home, this may be a rucksack or a mansion. Is it possible to create an architecture that stitches this tapestry of philosophy, aspiration, interest, movements, both seen and unseen, into a whole new landscape of enclosure and exposition, that changes in time and makes no distinction between art and architecture, no matter what "code" of aesthetics is being used? Can we create architectures that slip into other locations and spaces and return to show us what they've found and "plant" a notation of this event in our environment?

These "plantings" might exist for some for a long time, sometimes for shorter periods of time. Such ideas are capable of producing a sublimity of space that grows and decays, changes and rearranges, that speaks of the human condition as the actor in a series of linear, non-linear and quantum events. The torsions of everyday existence, small expansions, minute stresses and strain and stains, vibrations in the World Wide Web, tigers caged in the quantum zone, and many more, all have the potential to invigorate elements in this architecture.

There are precedents in Price's projects that have opened up ways for architects to appreciate and deal with these non-linear dynamics. These include scheduled demolition, expediency, subsumption algorithms where an architectural element might always seek to better its position, float or dream. Momentary connection devices in Price's work might take the form of a bridge, walkway or viewing tower; in my world they might be spatial wormholes or vacillating objects that flit across the actual and the virtual. Price and his collaborators taught architects cybernetic notions about systems of feedback and their archit-ectural potentials that include a building's self awareness, the weaving of smartness into otherwise inert materials and the disolution of the tired old building as controlling edifice. This and so much more wrapped up in the leftist politics of liberation, equality and plain human dignity is Price's legacy to the architectural profession.

More than any other architect, Price has shown us the fundamental importance of time. His work unflinchingly battles with the fixed entrenched notions of traditional architects, town planners and urban designers and their stupid ideological boundaries. Solutions are often found in the interstitial areas between accepted modes of thinking. It is here where the potential of liberation from the sullen objects we build around us to mitigate short lived problems can be cultivated. In *Cedric Price - The Square Book*[1], under a sketch of a GENERATOR module, Price has written "don't forget the undersides". It is precisely this quality of the unseen, the invisible and the barely revealed that underpins our assumptions about objects and space, and it is the manipulation of these that can be so emancipating.

As a young architect, I was like the kid who could play the guitar fast, everything was a pyrotechnic display of virtuosity: Cedric Price taught me to play the Blues.

3 — IDENTITY/IDENTIFICATION/CONTROL/PRIVATE, SECRET — SINGLE — DELIGHT

CELLULAR USE	PUBLIC LOCATIONAL	PRIVATE USAGE	VISUAL FIX	PERMANENT/ TEMPORARY	HISTORY DELIGHT	VISUAL IDENTITY	CONTROL SAFETY
X26 HOODHOLE	187 CITLIN	197 PORTHOLE	176 OBLIQUE	185 OXMAST	171 STARK	184 ASHMOLE	161 PERTHPAVS

NOT VERY IMPORTANT, EPHEMERA, SLIGHT, PARTICULAR, UNIQUE, LUXURY OF LAZINESS

LONG THOUGHTS

USE OF MEMORY

VALUE OF REMEMBERING

CASKETS OF MEMORY

CASKETS OF CONCEIT

SHORT RING

CONTAINMENT OF OTHERS' DELIGHTS

TEMPORARY DELIGHTS

SYMBOLS OF REALITY

3—

IDENTITY/ IDENTIFICATION/ CONTROL/ PRIVATE, SECRET— SINGLE— DELIGHT

161
PERTHPAVS

A pavilion for artworks owned by
Alistair McAlpine, in Australia. A square
timber construction is proposed, elevated
above water level by two large posts
and a single truss. The above ground
enclosure contains hinged showcases
which also serve to delineate access
and views out, with an obscured eye on
the water beneath through a floor-
mounted bris l'eau.

050

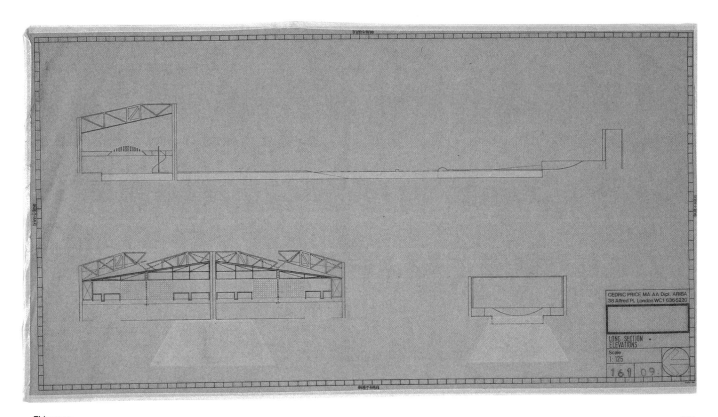

051

This page:

050. sketch view of pavilion.

*051. page of working drawings including long
section through pavilion and lake and a complex
exploded section to show both the angle of
the roof and the hand rails.*

184
ASHMOLE

A design for an exhibition called 'Ancient and Modern' at the Ashmolean Museum in Oxford. A double-sided display case (containing Neolithic axe heads and Iron Age braclets) is set diagonally across the room – an exercise in altering perspective. All objects are lit from behind emphasizing shape rather than detail. The case stands alone as its own object. It contains large batteries, rechargeable during periods of closure, thus avoiding wire trails from cabinet to wall sockets. The work of two artists and two architects is arranged around the four walls.

The following excerpt is from a review by Gerald Cadogan. The review was filed but never printed in the *Financial Times*.

"A barrage of flint axes, a stuffed chimpanzee swinging from a rope and a parade of sculpted heads hymn ancient themes in contemporary harmony with austere, bright abstracts by William Turnbull and the rich neo-Classicism of Quinlain Terry ...The scrum of 'Celtic' heads leads to Sidney Nolan's Celtic images, grey and black, fleshy and sensual.... Complementing the pictures and objects are Cedric Price's drawings for the 1982 competition for the National Gallery. The exhibition ...is a cornucopia of new and old art and craft that has spilt out of the collections of Lord McAlpine of West Green."

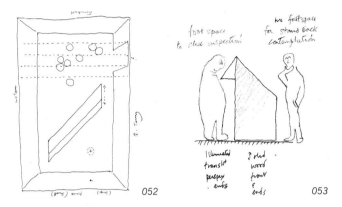

052   053

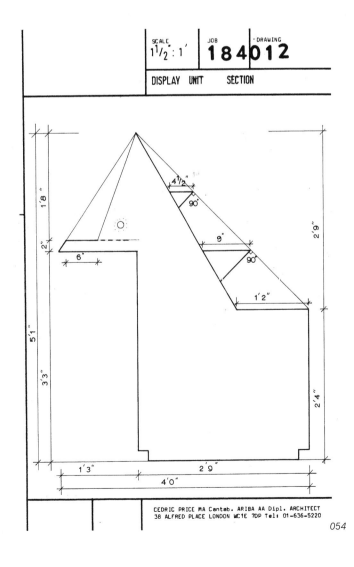

054

This page:

052. plan of exhibition space.
053. double-sided display unit.
054. section drawing of display unit.

185
OXMAST

In 1920 Lady Rhondda founded the political magazine *Time & Tide* which ran until 1977. With such distinguished writers amongst its archive, such as D.H.Lawrence, Virgina Woolf, George Bernard Shaw and George Orwell, Price contributed a design column that on one particular occasion discussed the joy of London's Regent Street Christmas Lights, in the pre-sponsorship-fairy-light era. Made of stamped out aluminium shapes they shook and rattled in the wind and caught the light from the permanent streetlamps.

A competition entry for the Oxford Street Christmas lights by CPA is based on some of these ideas. The brief specified that decorations must be fitted to the existing lamp standards and not attached to buildings. Competition judges included Norman Foster, Piers Gough, Sir Terence Conran, Vico Magistretti, Westminster Council leader Shirley Porter and Jim Braun, chairman of the Oxford Street Lights Committee.

Xmas competition for Oxford Street

OXFORD Street is planning to steal some of the limelight from this winter's Regent Street illuminations.

Traders are backing a design competition to revamp the street's ageing and paltry Christmas lights.

Designers, architects and engineers are being invited by the organiser, the Society of Industrial Artists & Designers, to submit a scheme for Christmas lighting that will run the 2km from Tottenham Court Road to Marble Arch.

The cost limit is approximately £50,000. Decorations must be fitted to the existing lamp standards and not attached to buildings.

The judges are Norman Foster, Piers Gough, Sir Terence Conran, Vico Magistretti, Westminster council leader Shirley Porter and Jim Braun, chairman of the Oxford Street Lights Committee. Prizes total £2,500, plus the commission.

Further details from Alastair Best, SIAD, 12 Carlton House Terrace, London SW1.

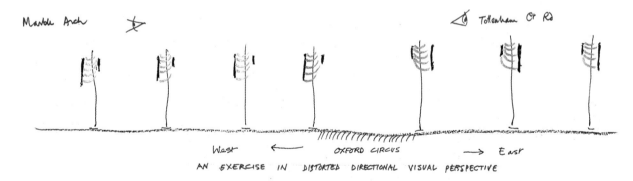

This page:

055. sketch propsal elevation and plan for Oxford Street highlighting the natural curve of the street.

176
OBLIQUE

An exercise in 'golden mean' taking the
form of a memorial for Alistair McAlpine's
father and located in the gardens of the
family home.

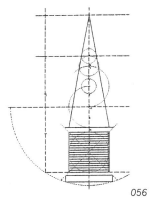

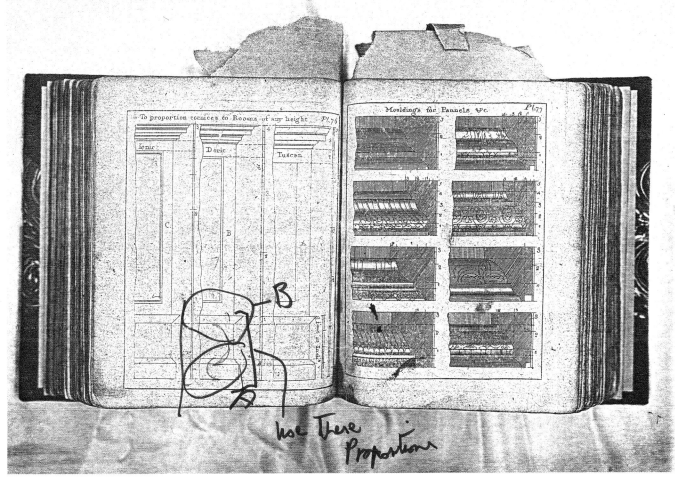

This page:

056. working drawing of OBLIQUE folly.

057. photocopy ref. page provided by client.

197
PORTHOLE

A commission from Lord Eliot, the present Earl St. Germans, for the grounds of Port Eliot, Cornwall. The site is precisely where the Earl's grandmother had located her own tent, built in the 1940s. Desiring a summer house she persuaded the National Health Service to 'prescribe' her one on account of her 'condition'. The prescribed structure rotated to catch the sun by means of a manually operated lever. In memory (of her bloody-mindedness) a lead tent was proposed, the material to be taken from the roof of the main house and melted down.

...of course follies are not useful – except, perhaps in making an awful mess of Anglo-Saxon puritanical rational standards.

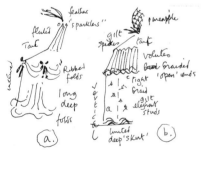

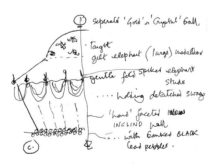

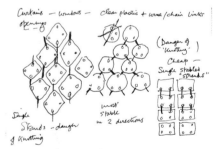

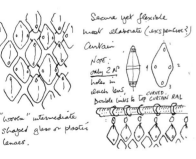

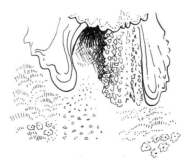

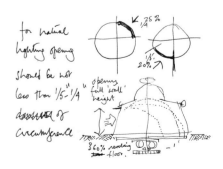

This page:
058. sketches of PORTHOLE folly with notes on material and fabrication methods.

X26
HOODHOLE

Adjustments to be made to a house belonging to a personal friend in order to raise that friend's spirits about, what CPA considered to be, a rather dreary little house. See adjacent remarks extracted from a two page written proposal.

- Open up all the main room.
- Use both outside areas in conjunction with this room.
- Planting of semi-mature trees this autumn should be considered.
- The big room be so furnished as to enable you to eat in any of the three areas.
- The fire should be reinstated (in Kit's Suite) and your favourite chair installed.
- Bathroom should be kept large and uncluttered.
- The guest bed(s) must be re-positioned.

SCALE	JOB	DRAWING
NTS	26	005

THE HOUSE & GARDEN

CEDRIC PRICE MA Cantab. ARIBA AA Dipl. ARCHITECT
38 ALFRED PLACE LONDON WC1E 7DP Tel: 01-636-5220

This page:

059. cutaway sketch linking house to garden.

187
CITLIN

"Berlin-Denkmal oder Denkmodell?":
an exhibition for ideas for the
start of the 21st century by 80
international architects.

Frank Mielchien was assistant on
this project. A former East-Berliner, he
worked as a taxi driver in Berlin for 6
months of the year to earn enough money
to return to work at CPA.

For good and bad reasons Berlin is now a superbly
unbalanced city. Demographically, geographically, socially and
economically it is uneven. Moves to make it a balanced
community should be resisted and reversed. The value of the
21st century city is the constructive unbalance that can be
achieved in the activities, services and resources it offers
to its citizens. Most world cities, uncertain of their future,
try desperately to accommodate all, limit population,
preserve the ancient fabric, revitalize 19th century services
and create a balanced society. Such cities are accelerating
their death. Berlin's future prosperity and delight will
only be achieved by harnessing and exploiting uncertainty and
encouraging unbalance.

Berlin has the educational and cultural dispensing equipment
for a city five times its size. It is also physically finite,
devoid of suburban sprawl and with regional links whose
lengths are less important than the speed of exchange that
they enable. People and ideas become multi-directional and
Berlin the human servicing station. The city of the future
must process people, enriching them with skills, capabilities
and appetites which can be exercised elsewhere for the rest
of their lives. A city can be a wonderful place to pass
through and a dreadful place to die. Architecture can nurture
new awareness and develop appetites but does not itself create
a culture – it is merely its by-product. Thus these proposals
by hinting at the unique quality of Berlin as gateway to a
better life have in themselves through example to encourage
the appetite for life-long progression and change. The
Triumphal Roman Arches of North Africa established both the
expanding Roman domain and the path to Rome. These four new
portals are aids to those who wish to use and enjoy the city
in order to leave enriched. They are reminders to those who
stay put. The portals are clearly numbered indicating the four
year period which is considered the ideal time span for
Berlin's special magic. Each Annual Portal should enable
additional accessibility to or utilization of the appropriate
humane servicing Berlin provides. The four sites vary as the
city "know-how" and metropolitan sophistication of the user
increases. Thus Portal One is obvious, Portal Four is near
the airport – the way out. The encouragment to use the city
as a launching pad rather than a Mecca will not only avoid
its life-span being prolonged unduly but also prove rewarding
to those who stay around.

060

This page:
060. schematic sketch of one of
the proposed Berlin gateways.
Opposite:
061. plan showing sequence of arrival of
all gateways in Berlin.
062. sketch of assembly and disassembly
of a gateway.
063. detail of type of services contained
within a gateway.
064. sketch view.

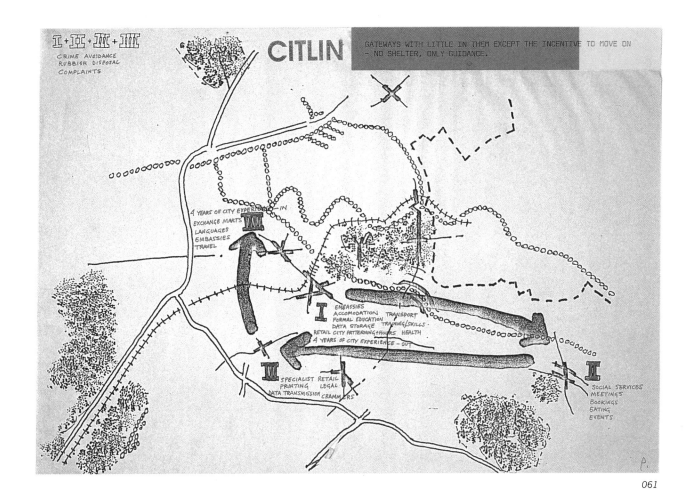

I + II + III + IIII
CRIME AVOIDANCE
RUBBISH DISPOSAL
COMPLAINTS

CITLIN

GATEWAYS WITH LITTLE IN THEM EXCEPT THE INCENTIVE TO MOVE ON — NO SHELTER, ONLY GUIDANCE.

4 YEARS OF CITY EXPERIENCE - IN
EXCHANGE MARTS
LANGUAGES
EMBASSIES
TRAVEL

I
EMBASSIES
ACCOMODATION   TRANSPORT
FORMAL EDUCATION
DATA STORAGE   TRAINING/SKILLS
RETAIL CITY PATTERNING+HOURS HEALTH
4 YEARS OF CITY EXPERIENCE - OUT

III
SPECIALIST RETAIL
PRINTING   LEGAL
DATA TRANSMISSION CRAMMERS

II
SOCIAL SERVICES
MEETINGS
BOOKINGS
EATING
EVENTS

061

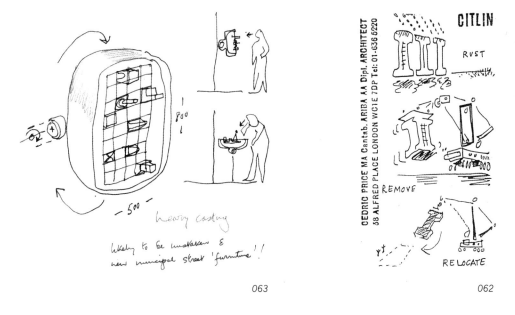

- 500
heavy casting
likely to be mistaken &
new municipal street 'furniture'!!

063

CEDRIC PRICE MA Cantab. ARIBA AA Dipl. ARCHITECT
38 ALFRED PLACE LONDON WC1E 7DP Tel: 01-636 6220

CITLIN
RUST

REMOVE

RELOCATE

062

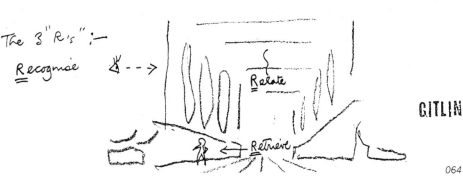

The 3 "R's":-
Recognise
Relate
Retrieve

CITLIN

064

4 — SHELTER & CONTAINMENT

OLD OIL AND OLD LAMPS – THE MIX MAKES THE DIFFERENCE

PROPOSITION OF THE ORDINARY – APPROXIMATION OF AS FOUND

203 ARKAGE	154 BRUNSWICK	153 VAUXHALL	188 FRANKFURT 206 BERLIN' 92 179 SKI	174 CONGRESS	194 TIFF
		HOUSE WORKING – OFFICE WORKING ANONYMOUS CLIENTS		FAMILIAR SPACE	THE CITY AS A MANTLE SHELF
COMMUNITY – NOW & NOT SO NEW					
CHANGE OF MIND	SLEIGHT OF HAND			ANONYMOUS SPACE – NEW GAME	
			NEW ? MIX	NEW ? LOCATION	NOW U SEE IT NOW U DON'T
DELIGHT – USEFULNESS					
PARTICULARISATION OF THE SITE	IDENTITY THROUGH ACTIVITY	INDIVIDUAL APPETITES	DISPLAY SECURITY DIFFICULTY OF ACCESS UNIQUENESS		"THE ENCLOSURE BUSINESS"

4 –

SHELTER
AND
CONTAINMENT

194
TIFF

Competition entry for a new Tokyo Forum building, Japan. Price's fascination is with a site that presents a typical Tokyo condition, i.e. that of a very crowded site:

a) volumetrically – to be visually comprehensible to all.

b) operationally and logistically – allowing for "operational slack".

c) structurally – in order to meet earthquake regulations.

"The Cedric Price Forum entry looks to the articulation of contemporary obsessions. As the castellations of medieval fortifications emphasized defence, the chimneys of the later manor houses boasted of the luxury of fireplaces, Price makes a virtue of the escape routes and stairs required stringent Japanese safety regulations. Visitors rise from the underground into a huge ground floor/level one concourse. Here, a network of internal streets provides information and eating facilities. The floor above, the "deck/level two", creates a partly sheltered plaza, from which all cultural zones can be reached. The auditoria and exhibition halls lie above these two levels, in three major subdivisions. The separation of activities enables whole zones to operate independently and enforces acoustic control. The circulation spine runs north to south, articulated by a self-supporting light-weight structure. Price orientates the Forum towards the railway (unlike the majority of entrants who envisage the main entrance from the existing main road though the business district) and the adjoining cultural area of Ginza – a more logical and natural neighbour."

"Tokyo Revisited", BD, 8 December 1989.

The plan for the main plaza level is a slice in time, only useful in relation to above and below. Having resolved the level I could then grow vegetables... a rare and peculiar vegetable garden. The scale and simplicity of these major forms is intended to serve as an initial signing of the variety of uses and services available to all.

This page:
065. sketches of and about TIFF with notes.
Opposite:
066. diagrammatic section.
067. isometric with comparative plans to indicate scale.
068. sketch describing R.Buckminster Fuller's observation about "fancy-nozzles", being that if one were to take a high pressure hose to a typical U.S. residential area and wash away all the earth surrounding the bases of all the houses one would be left with "nothing more than fancy nozzles [the houses] linked by the pipe networks".
069. ground floor/level one plan – a plan with which Price is particularly pleased.

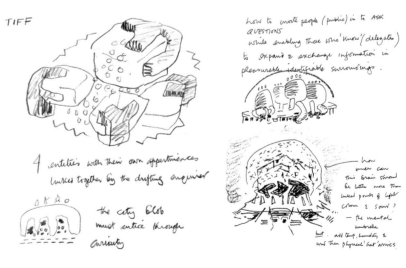

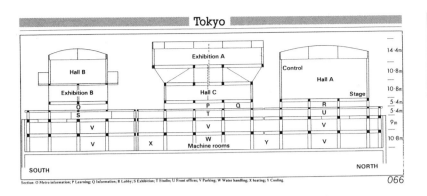

Tokyo

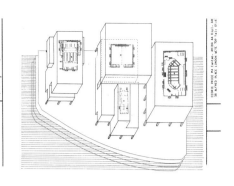

TIFF

"fancy nozzles" R.B-F.

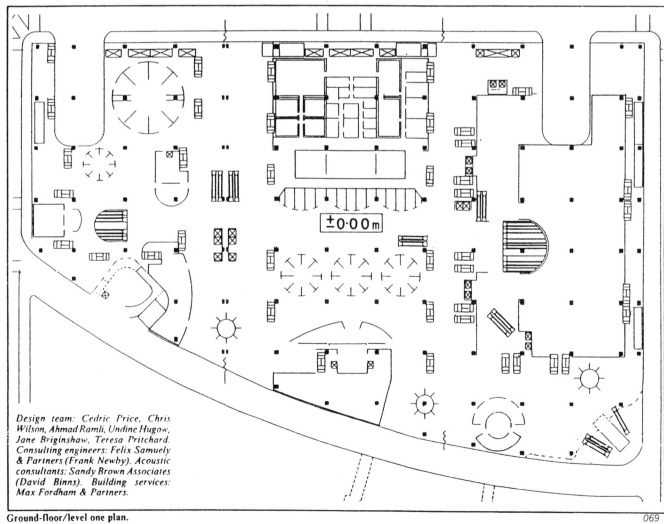

Design team: Cedric Price, Chris
Wilson, Ahmad Ramli, Undine Hugow,
Jane Briginshaw, Teresa Pritchard.
Consulting engineers: Felix Samuely
& Partners (Frank Newby). Acoustic
consultants: Sandy Brown Associates
(David Binns). Building services:
Max Fordham & Partners.

Ground-floor/level one plan.

188
FRANKFURT

The adjacent excerpts are from a report written by CPA for the University of Frankfurt.

Because it isn't going to be pulled down, generally speaking its going to be there – so it's a question of breathing new life.

Voluntary Higher Education has established a language of enablement in Europe. The opportunity for student choice in subject matter is now being matched by the increasing agreement and capacity by facilities not only to share information and resources but to establish the opportunity for entire new academic disciplines to be established. This design brief encourages investigation of where the built environment can enable such change.

Any proposed design strategy and its resultant built tactics must become a four-dimensional essay on opportunity, a précis on change and primer on operation. These proposals must create a built environment that encourages future change and that do not deter people from changing their mind. Thus many of these proposals are designed to establish, in built form, calculated uncertainty.

PROPOSALS

Activities: New developments must provide the capacity for well-serviced volumes (three-dimensional spaces) before the particular protective volume (building) is provided. The volumes within old buildings are often more valuable to maintain than the most recent telephone, lavatory or restaurant.

Movement: the Frankfurt underground railway system is an ideal feed to and from the University and provides ideal links to other centres of activity. The U-Bahn should be seen as an extension of the University in providing information in the stations and the trains both for students and outsiders. The notice board is often too late. The availability of off-site parking of bicycles and vehicles should result from city planning traffic decisions – not from University pressure groups. The University in a City is urbanely particular. (A floating university in Japan is having problems with the navigation authorities.)

Information & Exchange: the University's combined data stores and their capacity for retrieval should be seen as a major resource for both the students and the city community. The availability of information on work being undertaken in the University is a major resource for the city. Four information globes, easily visible and accessible from the main road, 'self-service' electronic information billboards incorporated in the three major cross route entries into the new extended campus: seven information and exchange points should all contain normal telephone facilities and city services, data banks and eventually replace the existing public telephone

Page 066:
070a, b, c. the capacity for linkages.
Page 067:
071. plan of Frankfurt University and town centre with notes in English – final proposal presented in German.

kiosks in the area. The conventional remote enquiry desk - often unmanned, is no longer a sufficient service

Community amenities: the availability of refreshment should be seen as a service throughout the Campus and largely available to the public - a general food market established in this area. The availability of printing and photographic services, sale of books, audio and video tapes, student equipment, banks, chemists, travel agents and clothiers should all be encouraged on the understanding 'That which the University Buys' - becoming a valuable advertisement of the rest of Frankfurt. The University Health Service should establish a public health clinic providing advice, at least, to the local community.

Use of existing/listed buildings: the peculiarities of these buildings should be accentuated particularly in relation to the quality of interior spaces. The nocturnal image of the University must be visible from aircraft and from the increasing number of tall buildings in Frankfurt. The immediate thresholds and doorways of such buildings should be scrupulously clean - always. The presence of the Museum in the middle of the University should be visually celebrated and treated as a living/working "casket of jewels". "Internal" demolition of several buildings is essential.

New buildings & structures: all new buildings should be three floors high. Such a building requires a simple structure, the minimum of lifts and is easy to demolish.

Landscape: trees should be confined to the south, east and western boundries of the site and retained between the houses...healthy existing trees should be retained, the rest felled and new trees planted. Ground cover should be flowering shrubs and not allowed to grow higher than 3m. All ivies should be excluded. Uniformity of colour of flowering shrubs should be maintained - in the red range of the spectrum. Perfumed plants should predominate. "Street litter" should be removed. This includes telephone kiosks, sculpture, low level lighting. New stone and concrete haunching should be installed against the edge of buildings facilitating pavement cleaning. Artificial lighting is extremely important - related to particular routes. All free standing lighting is to be removed and a high level accessible tension network installed, capable of supporting seasonal lighting, flags, banners and other temporary displays. Water should be reintroduced to the site in the form of a shallow rapid flowing stream of 'moat' around the entire perimeter of the site with appropriate 'bridges'. Paintwork (gloss cream in specified areas) should be continually cleaned and repainted.

Main zones & cross road: the surface of this entire area is an enormous design programme. Sudliches Erweiterungsgelande: new three-storey building and rehabilitation of AFE-Turm. Robert-Mayer Strasse: should be a university parking street. Grundungsgelände:museum extension demolished. 'Community information gateway' on Grafstrasse. Chimney replaced by a flagpole of the same height - the City indicator. Mertonstrasse: main university avenue to be constantly cleaned. Forumgelände: partial demolition would create the largest civic space in Frankfurt extending from Mertonstrasse across Bockenheimer Landstrasse to beyond the Depothalle. New building to define northern limit of campus. Bockenheimer Landstrasse & Depotgelände: the University City Mall. Throughout the site a system of foul weather protection - not necessarily structures - must be devised.

The urban quality of the University must be readily recognizable even to those who have no interest in its academic industry. This allotted area should never be extended - in physical terms. Future growth must require further demolition - for which there is much potential material. The growth of any University in non-physical terms depends on the quality of its source generation.

FRANKFURT 188

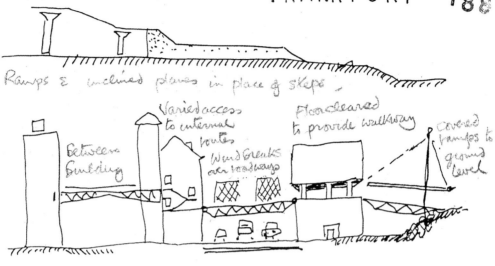

Ramps & inclined planes in place of steps.

Varied access to external routes

Floor cleared to provide walkway

Covered ramps to ground level

Between building

Wind breaks over roadways

THE CAPACITY FOR LINKAGES

070a

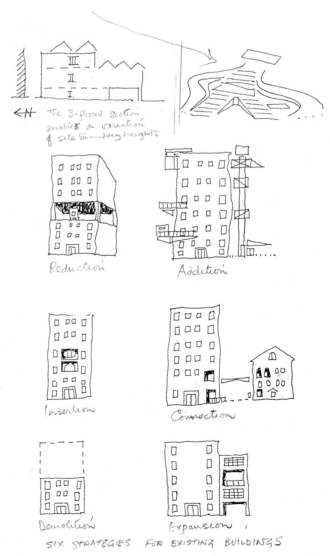

←N The 3-floored section enables a variation of site boundary heights

Reduction

Addition

Insertion

Connection

Demolition

Expansion

SIX STRATEGIES FOR EXISTING BUILDINGS

070c

a blanket of learning
warm - tucked in time
snug - folded removed
spread generously

elsewhere.

188

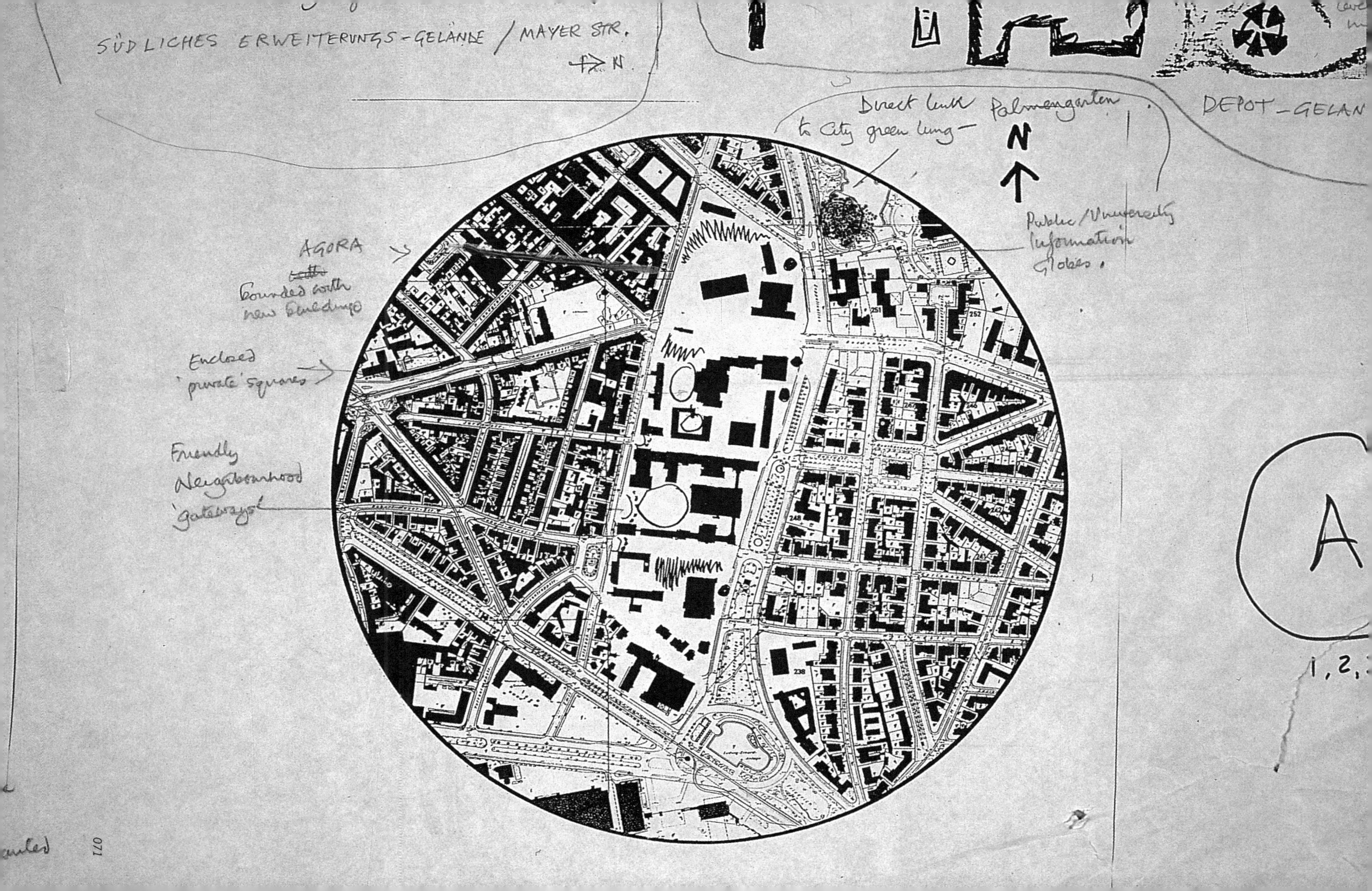

SÜDLICHES ERWEITERUNGS-GELÄNDE / MAYER STR.

⇨ N.

DEPOT-GELÄN

N ↖

Direct link Palmengarten
to City green lung —

Public/Municipal
Information 'kiosks'

AGORA →

Bounded with
new Buildings

Enclosed
'public squares' →

Friendly
Neighbourhood
'Gateways'

A

1, 2, 1

206
BERLIN' 92

Welltempered Architecture – Concepts for Green Office Buildings: a design workshop, of seven teams comprising students, architects and environmental engineers working on seven sites around Berlin to develop buildings that combine a minimum energy consumption with a high architectural standard. The projects were displayed at the Aedes Galerie, Berlin.

One team comprises Cedric Price, Max Fordham, Almut Ernst, Katharina von Ehren, Christopher McCarthy with students Peter Baumgartner, Ayse Hicsasmaz, Susanne Knoop, Jan Liesegang, Katharina Maske, Christoph Mayer, Andreas Munch, Barbara von Raffay, Barbara Schultz, Christof Struhk, Gunnar Tausch and Susanne Wachsmann. Their site is a 750 m length of 16 year old, but never used, Autobahn running above ground level (a bridge without a use). Using this as the foundation (with its in-built power supplies) the office takes on a linear nature, drawing in material at one end and emitting its product at the other. The cross feeds onto the motorway from housing are ideally fitted for workers to access at any point along its length. A light-weight sleeve forms the enclosure, its section comprising two zones: the outer buffer zone has bright light or temperatures above 5 degrees C, providing a multi-purpose work area. The inner spinal zone has a heavy weight translucent ceiling (water filled glass planks) designed to store surplus energy and balance the heat flow over 24 hours. Due to 24 hour operation, the energy consumption is 1/20 of a comparable conventional office building whilst the construction energy is halved.

The introduction to the exhibition catalogue, written by Philipp Oswalt and Florian Kossak states:
"Besides the subject of energy saving other questions arose during the workshop in connection with chosen building type: what (re)presents an office today....In order to design an office building one had to define the workplace of the future. Our idea to concentrate on the building function does not mean to optimize a specific use. The use is not defined, its change not predictable. To build functional is to allow for a variety of uses. To build functional is not to optimize a specific function, but to provide comfort. This is the key to the understanding of the title."

A reasonable application of an air structure...

The application of smart structures and materials to architecture must occur at the concept stage of design ...because SS&M introduce TIME as an essential fourth dimension in the very definition of their usefulness. Due to previously assumed incompatability of the measurement of TIME with that of the normal architectural dimensions of length, breadth, height and weight, TIME has remained idle on such questions of 'ageing' or redundancy.

Paper presented at the Second European Conference on Smart Structures and Materials, Glasgow, 1994. ed. by A. McDonald et al., Smart Structures Research Institute. Spie Volume 236.

*Additional ref. Tom Porter, **Architectural Drawing Masterclass**, Studio Vista, 1993.*

072

This page:
072. photocopy collage of photographed model.

179
SKI

A preliminary report commissioned by the Norwegian government "on what to look for in a business park in a marvellous site just outside Oslo, Norway – the end use of which I would know nothing about". The report by CPA comprises a survey of existing business parks in the U.K. including Stockley Park, the U.K.'s largest business park at that time. CPA cites amongst that project's assets a London telephone number – an 18 hole golf course, a 'build-one leave – one' basis of development, pavilion type buildings sited in a bowl around lakes, 250 acres of landscaped grounds and leases available for small tenants.

The report also cites the Southbank Polytechnic London Science Park: Engineering & Technology- "Technopark" which holds a unique centre-city site and only three storey high buildings with linking balconies. (ref. FRANKFURT).

Siting is the key to [CPA's] list of recommendations in order to recognise the peculiarty of the site and exploit it... enabling the visitor to comprehend quickly the nature and size of the site. Seasonal visual changes should be realised. The use of grid layout on an uneven site increases the clarity of the layout.

Ref. to DETROIT THINK-GRID introducing a communal, 'experimental' floor throughout the park.
A unique centre for labour relations and union management experimentation – a prototype skill park.

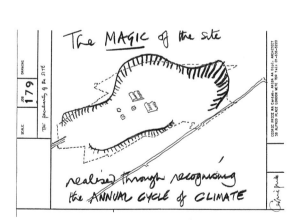

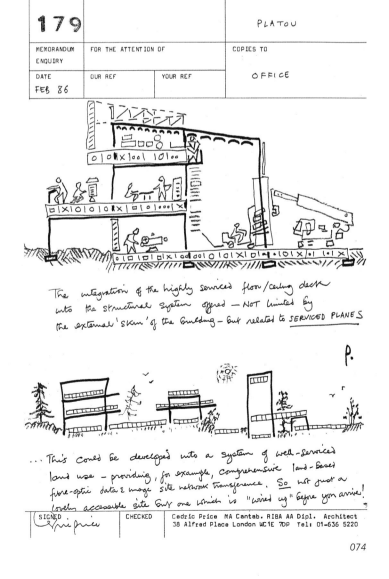

This page:
073. "the magic of the site", nr. Oslo.
074. sketch sections of "serviced planes".

154
BRUNSWICK

A commission to carry out a feasibility
study with examples of how to reactivate
the Brunswick Centre, Bloomsbury,
London, originally designed by Patrick
Hodgkinson, 1959-72.

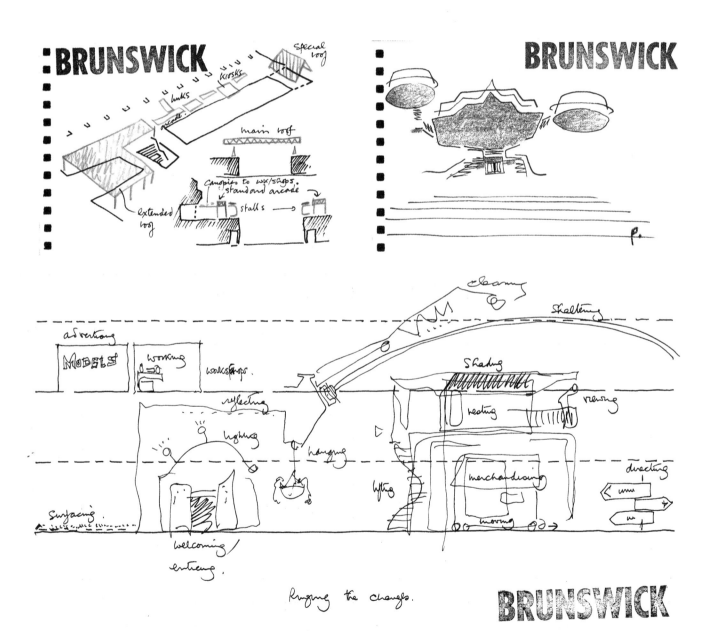

203
ARKAGE

A competition for a new town, Arkwright, on the site of former coal mines. The competition was advertised at the time when the National Coal Board began to undergo privatization leaving little hope for a coherent, cohesive or continuous approach to the development of this new town.

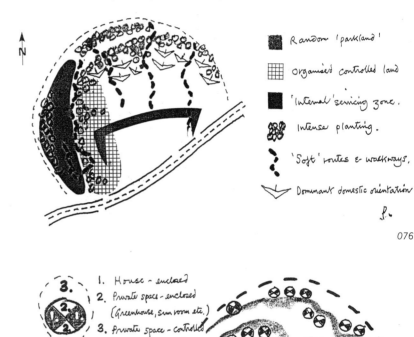

076

077

076. despite a prolonged site visit it is premature to produce anything more than this simple diagram of relationships.
077. domestic domains. This office considers it essential for user/client and designer discussion on free-will activities and desirable futures to precede such (conceptual) design work. These diagrams show merely the relationships of enclosures, enclosed space and open space of private household. Maximum usage of most community areas is desirable. Shared volumes, services and equipment where feasible should, through detailed design, enable 7 day a week usage for a high number of hours.

KESTER RATTENBURY

—

*Kester Rattenbury trained as an architect and completed a PhD on the intrinsic bias of architectural coverage in the UK press, before becoming an architectural journalist. She has worked extensively as a writer and reviewer for **Building Design** and for other UK national papers, architectural magazines and books since 1990. Most recently she compiled and edited **This Is Not Architecture** (Routledge, 2002). Rattenbury currently teaches design at the University of Westminster.*

Strange (but Optimistic) Fruit.

Thinking about Cedric Price's work is like trying to walk up a mountain (and that with a hangover). It is at the edge of what you think you might possibly be able to do; more than you assume you can imagine. You are off the marked paths and out of the normal boundaries. You might get stuck, or scared, or make a fool or yourself, or trip over something simple. But if you can cope, even for a while, you'll get views that you have never seen before and you will never forget.

Trying to write about him always feels to me like walking the plank. You know that you are dealing with ideas that are unprecedented – not in their sources, which are simply very unusual, but in the conjunction of those sources, and in the propositions generated. You are also dealing with ideas that are – usually – visually unimaginable. ("It will probably look," Reyner Banham said of the FUN PALACE, "like nothing on earth"[1]). At least, they would look like nothing you might think of as architecture: a pile of containers, a building site, some railway tracks and carriages.

You cannot imagine or describe Price's work using the shortcut of visual predictions on which so much architectural journalism depends – and which most people imagine is its main point. Unlike almost any other architect's work, if your first reaction is to imagine what it looks like, you have probably missed the point. You cannot sell it to editors based on images either (getting MAGNET into the *Guardian*[2] was an effort of sheer trust on the commissioning editor's part). And you know that you are describing work that is dauntingly influential.

Writing Price.

I first came across Price when I was a trainee journalist on *Building Design* in 1990: *BD* editor Paul Finch always invariably late, elated and full of extraordinary pieces of information from the weekly brandy breakfasts with "the mythical Cedric". The elegantly cynical *BD* buildings editor John Welsh returned from a stargazing student event with Price in Croatia (which went on to influence the TURTLAN project) – unwontedly half-enchanted. There was an endless tension with *BD's* excellent sub-editors who were not allowed to touch Price's unorthodox monthly column copy[3]. The glorious rebellion when the chief sub, late at night at the *BD* 150th anniversary, told him what she thought of his copy-writing habits, while he admired the haircut which showed the tips of her ears.

So to be asked to write about MAGNET a few years later was an alarming honour. It took several goes, as I remember; maybe three mornings sitting in East Grinstead – the white room at the top of Price's late Alfred Place office – with brandy, very strong coffee and slightly withered fruit – talking about things of extraordinary scope whose relationship was not altogether clear. And surrounded by masses and masses of sheets of paper; diagrams and notes and drawings, none of them having the definitive, single key-image status for which the journalist is trained to look. Comparative studies on the sizes of buses and cathedrals, for instance; information on scissor jack lifts; walking distances from ten different sites: grainy, diagrammatic photo-montages – and those were only the most closely descriptive images; the ones we actually chose. And, struggling all the time to think how I could describe it; this collection of ten, different, temporal, unlike devices.

Some seemed sweet as ice-cream (the viewing platform through the trees over the zoo). Some had a toughness which gradually took hold of your mind as both deeply political and deeply poetic (the sliding town square which would link the severed housing and cause those grim houses next to the North Circular Road to be demolished). Some were more difficult: cheeky, intrusive, almost claustrophobic (I only really "got" the pleasure of the over-looking through the enjoyment of my neighbours scaffolding), or awkward, like the library bridge in Milton Keynes.

I imagine the library bridge was toughest for me to describe because it connected to a realm of Price projects which I did not then know too well (except, of course, by reputation): the FUN PALACE and POTTERIES THINKBELT. These, like many other Price projects, effectively propose new kinds of anti-institutions; where flexible, demountable and non-precious structures become temporary agents of new sites and activities – sometimes very large and complex ones. MAGNET – which now makes its first appearance in book form – has entered the realm of these great but arcane projects.

Built or unbuilt.

Price is prescient – a status confirmed by the support he has had from engineers who are amongst his strongest supporters – and serious clients like British Rail, even if they don't necessarily have the courage to follow through. All of his work is peppered with ideas and sites that he has picked up long before anyone else – and of course, many more which are still to be picked up. His hugely catholic scope allows him to notice things that the rest of us (the profession ?) are resolutely determined to miss – our limitation, our loss. In his Price Cuts in the *AJ*[4], for instance, he predicted the critical problem of flooding ages ago; in 1996 he predicted a foot and mouth outbreak in 2000+. He's a Cassandra with suggestions.

This influence extends to a whole series of generations of buildings of astonishing range. Price's overt influence on the Pompidou Centre is well documented[5]; but other projects less so. He has a nose for a critical site like no-one else: just check this book through for sites that other people have or will pick up. His was the first – and most radical and best – scheme for the post 1970s redevelopment of London's much maligned South Bank. Unlike all those who were to follow him, Price's SOUTH BANK proposed more open space, not less. "London's last lung", he called it. Typically – heretically – he proposed bridging over a huge swathe of the Thames – forming a huge public square with public facilities around it – amongst them, details of an underground railway opening onto the river, the "Thing" on the site of what is now the Imax Cinema and, modestly, a big wheel with observation capsules on the Jubilee Gardens site. Price is not yet widely credited with having provided the direct inspiration for the London Eye, though he confirms that Marks Barfield have acknowledged it.

The relation between Price's work and what actually is built is particularly interesting because Price himself has built little. This is not surprising. He famously ignored the profession's self-supporting and absolute credo that the answer is always a building. He will tell his clients instead that they need a computer, a car, or a divorce (hardly the modesty he always advocates, as Charles Jencks has pointed out*[6]). And he overturns the profession's other great unspoken credo – that the architect's greatest responsibility lies in an aesthetic that will last into the unforseeable future. His built work simply does not fit into the glossy publications that form such a huge structural part of our construction of professional value and worth. Price instead argues that our responsibility is to anticipate change, to offer new possibilities – and to know exactly when and how the things that we have put up can be taken away again. His analogies with food are partly based on the idea that we all seem to eat far more than we can digest.

Aesthetic or delight.

Trying to fit Price's buildings into our normal, visual first and foremost aesthetic assessment system never quite works. His aesthetic is a curious thing. The INTER-ACTION building, recently demolished (Price told listing officers it should certainly be pulled down) really was a frame with Portacabins. The AVIARY: oddly lovable, dramatic, effective in its landscape, yet somehow not normally glamorous. Of the many unbuilt schemes, the aesthetic – what we would normally call the architecture – varies hugely – and comes through relationships and situations that take a lot of thinking through. IFPRI – another 'city lung', this time in the middle of Manhattan – seemed beautiful first by imagining its grid of blue glass balls under the snow. From this, it was somehow easier to imagine the joy of the big, rough open space with the fresh air blowing off the Hudson[7]. Other projects – like STRATTON or HALMAG – can look almost brutally unaesthetic: hardly architecture at all, we might think if we drove past.

The delight that Price advocates is often, at least partly, invisible – or at least difficult to predict or pinpoint in architectural pictures. Maybe its best imitators give us some idea of this: the old, free ride up the escalators in the Pompidou. Or the beauty of the London Eye – when so many of us critics had nothing good to say of it until it was up – the astonishment of its structure, its views, and incidentally its temporary status, became unexpectedly, gloriously obvious. Since little of Price's work is built, it requires that leap of imagination to see, for instance, SOUTH BANK not as an heretical covering of riverside but as the greatest bridge and public space in t he world. This delight lies in the activity, the view, the possibility, the facility, the opportunity. The object itself does not have the religious status that our professional culture generally invokes. In this, and almost uniquely, he denies us the addictive tendency we have to trap the world in inappropriate and inflexible solutions because we have built without knowing how to take away again – and we have built in a way which

means we love the aesthetic object more than the kind of activity it offers. In many ways, Price evades the trap of the aesthetic altogether.

In Re:CP*[8], Rem Koolhaas argues that Price wilfully suppresses and downplays his aesthetic. He points out that his minimal drawings convey the bare minimum but absolute accurate idea; his drawings and handwriting absolutely define their own "awkward beauty". Again, with few built examples, it is difficult to test this. It is notable that the refitted Pompidou Centre, was enslaved to and evicted by its physical beauty: now a pay to view zone and painted, for some inconceivable reason, white. The aesthetic object has been valued over the activity, the function; those functions have been pushed out the door while the residual building camouflages their departure. This could not happen with the FUN PALACE; take away the action and nothing recognisable as architecture remains.

The usefulness of the iconoclast within.

I've always found it – partly – amazing that Price is so hugely respected and loved by the profession since he so entirely overturns what we like to assume that architecture is. He does not just cut his way out of the corral of self-constructed aesthetic reassurance, of familiar novelties and known beauties or familiar iconoclasms. He attacks it like a charging rhino. He proposes, more or less single-handedly, a different way of thinking, a different kind of responsibility; one of activity and possibility. Koolhaas and Jencks have raised a slightly different argument, the faint chimera of something else, an underlying, aesthetic; the immodesty of telling someone to get a divorce, the lateral thought and residual conscience of what is, after all, a resolutely immodest profession. It is a welcome, small, viaticum of maybe-truth to help us see some of the trails Price is cutting way off outside our lazily constructed confines of how the profession might think, what it might notice and what it might do.

JANE BRIGINSHAW

—

Jane Briginshaw is a practising architect, lecturer in architecture, former Labour Councillor, Parliamentary candidate and candidate in London for the European Parliamentary elections of 2004. TIFF was the main project that she participated in during her time working as a recent graduate in the offices of Cedric Price Architects.

Architects in the fast lane.

This design reaches beyond the formal qualities of architecture to deal with the quality of urban life. Mr. Price's chief concern, very simply, is with public health. It aims to improve the air, the amount of available light and the psychological release that open space provides. It is, in effect, a park in which the archaeology of the industrial city takes the place of pastoral landscaping.

Mr. Price's "lung" essentially treats the site as a rectangular nature preserve. Train tracks would remain uncovered. New development would be banned. Over time some existing buildings would be eliminated. The site would be marked with a sparkling covering composed of small glass spheres.

No massive new construction. No sports stadiums. No urban bone crunching. No high-tech structural calisthenics. No hay to be made. Just a light dusting of glass frosting and a breeze blowing from the river. Just a place for a city to breathe[1].

Herbert Muschamp's description of Cedric Price's competition submission for the redevelopment of a huge strip of land on the West Side of New York, "The Lung for Midtown Manhattan" (IFPRI), sits alongside projects such as DUCKLANDS, FRANKFURT, the POTTERIES THINKBELT and WESTPEN representing the best of his tangential brilliance; funny, ordinary mixtures, so difficult to describe, yet presenting an ocean of possibilities. It is Price's desire to create his designs without limit that has driven him to be widely informed and enter into the fields of government and politics. It is his fascination by all things and people that has brought him to those designs.

Price demands that we step beyond the zone where mastery of building is the sole ambition. He is architect as opinionated leader and campaign manager. In 1995, MAGNET proposed fresh incursions into realms not usually inhabited by the architect. The project is located in ten different metropolitan sites. Sites that are eminently suitable and usable, except that no-one has asked an architect to build on them. Using short life structures occurring between urban spaces, taking in stairways, walkways, elevators, arcades and piers, the architect suggests that his work may (rather than should) change the way we use the city. This attitude is central to Price's practice of architecture, secure in a firm social responsibility. His prophetic calls on the architectural profession to shoulder this type of social responsibility for fear of being marginalised have largely come true. Part of the reason why MAGNET and other such projects are not given due attention by the profession and then fail to be taken up by government is because the former is seen to have no interest in the daily concerns of people. Price is providing a solution to a question that nobody asked him to ask – surely this is exactly where the architect/citizen's duty lies.

"architects, never in the fast lane, need to do the forward thinking for society if they are to avoid being left to pick up the pieces of shy decisions and choices: that unless the architectural body takes things in hand… the nature of the decisions that we make will become less and less worthwhile to society[2]."

For Price, change is beneficial. Just as any politician when asked why they have embarked on such a career would reply "Why, it was to change the world", so Price's political engagement is no secret. Financially supporting his brother at a young age after his own father's death may have helped Price develop a solid and unswerving political commitment. Norman Willis, TUC General Secretary between 1984 and 1993 and with whom he was close friends from the late 1970s describes Price as "cheerful Leftish Labour, who was pained and critical of those who drifted right in later life… who was somewhere between never escaping strong and generous principles and never letting strong and generous principles escape him." Price's politics are not merely theoretical. His hilarious (sometimes devastating) election parties were the culmination of election campaigns aided by Price-designed Labour posters in every window of his central London office. His disbelief at Tony Blair's failure to grasp history, his unbelievable loyalty waiting up until 4am on election night to phone me for the results in the seat where I was standing. The seat was unwinnable for Labour in Surrey and really only important for me the candidate and local activists, but by following details in detail and with seriousness Price builds and feeds his knowledge of things and people and never static social systems.

He likes to talk to people. He reads avidly and is fiercely meticulous about storage of information for later use. Grist for projects so grounded in their practicality could only be generated by someone fascinated by the world and its people. What other point is there in being an architect? As Norman Willis says, one of the reasons why they remained such close friends was Cedric's unsentimental attitude towards the working classes. Price's architecture has no mawkish attachment to stylistic superficialities. It does not patronise or exploit; it serves people today with the needs of today and with a thought about tomorrow. As the 1961 FUN PALACE was the antithesis of a palace of culture so the 1999 project for the Sir John Soane Museum addressed the need for museums "as places of transitional dialogue and cultural production".

"The role of architecture as a provider of visually recognisable symbols of identity, place and activity becomes an increasingly attractive excuse for architects to revel in the immensity of their personal visual dexterity, aesthetic sensibility and spatial awareness …call it a fix or the image of a city…

in general, it is both incomprehensible and irrelevant.[3]"

Cedric Price's skill lies in designing buildable realisations of political ideas that contain implied criticisms and challenges. Taking the Magnets as an example, a team of Price people would sort out any questions in advance. Like a giant building-sized, pre-prepared meal kit with the oven warmed up already, investigations into all aspects of realisation including lifting, levelling, disassembly and demolition would have been carried out and for sale to appropriate government departments. All that would remain is to say yes and occupy the space.

So if there are no practical difficulties, the barrier to acceptance must be either in the idea or in the people with the power to say yes. Just suppose for a moment that MAGNET is proposed for implementation in David Miliband's South Shields constituency and it were to arrive on the desk of the Minister of State for School Standards tomorrow. What would he do? The project would have local relevance to the people he represents and it would attract publicity. The forty new areas for which Miliband has responsibility include Raising School Standards in Primary and Secondary schools, Overall Responsibility for Raising School Standards, Literacy and Numeracy Strategies, Specialist Schools, Beacon Schools, Academies, Indepen-dent Schools, Reform of Secondary Education and so on. In response to this daunting list, would not Price's proposals, which, *"through their form and content contain the social magnet for learning, information, sanctuary and delight"* be a balm and a godsend?

For a second you might believe it could happen. But do not think in a million years that David Miliband, Tony Blair's head of policy for seven years, enlightened young and imaginative as he is, would dream of touching it. Here lies the implied criticism. We have seen there are no practical problems and there

are no difficulties with common values. The problem is that David Miliband, like all his colleagues, is disciplined to stay within his boundaries, just as architects have agreed to stay within theirs. For a politician, raising school standards does not mean doing something vaguely improving because it is no longer possible to be vague or amateurish. In their anxiety to be held to account government speakers talk with great conviction and for the best reasons about things that can be measured and named. And because this approach leaves so much untackled it can only accept simplistic and limited solutions. "According to the OECD the variation in performance within schools is four times as great as the variation in performance between schools. The UK has one of the biggest class divides in education in the industrialised world. We need to address provision in school, provision out of school, and provision in the home and in the community.[4]"

There is no suggestion that by adopting MAGNET the government would solve education's problems overnight – this is not what Magnets do. But, they do provide a means for stepping outside of the government's self-imposed boundaries, and would therefore be helpful in making connections to richer long-term solutions.

With the courage to allow uncertainty to bear its unpredictable fruits academics and teachers might have embraced MAGNET, "The working referendum of the possibilities for change: provisional structures giving adjustable public access to unconsidered spaces, generators for new kinds of activity[5]". Today's politicians could not. Indeed, one can imagine their crass derision masking their internal failure to comprehend.

Miliband is part of a government that is, as Roy Hattersley puts it "clever but profoundly un-intellectual[6]". These men and women are earnest and energetic but they are neither imaginative nor romantic, no more able to embark on

open-ended adventures into unknown possibilities than they could dive for pearls. That may be a good thing, since our lives depend on them for so much. But, through remaining within the boundaries of what is accepted good practice and management of the country they may just be able to make some improvements by being a little more clever and a little more humane than their predecessors. Failure to be so must be the ultimate missed opportunity.

Price has never built alliances or conducted conventional campaigns. Indeed his diffidence does not permit it. To bemoan the fact that so many of the radical designs remain paper projects is to miss the point. The projects hold up a mirror to the poverty of our established ways. They illustrate time after time that poetry has practicality and in that built form could occupy the place that we generally inhabit.

Muschamp's commentary bears this out:

"The design probably never stood a chance of winning. It can't pass for practical. City officials had already defined the site as the city's next great development corridor. But the idea of practicality is completely relative in this context. None of the projects are officially authorised. None have clients. The quality they project is not reality, but rather realness, to employ a term coined by uptown drag queens. They are practicality impersonators, developers en travesti."

The current architectural establishment, many of whom are Price's own students, continue to pay lip service to him, and meanwhile has remained, as was alwaysthe case, the client's servants, the servant of money and sometimes art, but certainly not to society. Nothing radical here, no change there. How is it that the profession has never, with its new-found power and influence, had the desire to fight for the ultimate proof of its admiration?

5 – MAKING SENSE OF CHANGING ENDS BY ALTERING MEANS

RETHINKING COMMUNICATIONS

CHANGING PRIORITIES RATED IN THE PAST

ACTION AND INTERACTION

216 APPEX

192 NEWLINK

195 CONTROL

205 RINK

190 STRATE II

183 STRATE I

DESIGN SEDATIVES
A REAL DRAWING

ACCEPTING THE MIX OF TIME

"BAND-AIDS"
DISGUISED AS
CONVENIENCE

MOVEMENT
TIME OF MOVEMENT
DURATION
FIXING OF TARGETS
DURABILITY OF NETWORK
PHASING – RE-PHASING
DURABILITY OF CONTROL
CHANGE THROUGH TIME
CONTINUOUS RETHINK
CONTINUITY
ENRICHMENT THROUGH REUSE

5–

MAKING SENSE OF CHANGING ENDS BY ALTERING MEANS

183/190
STRATE 1/2

Together, projects 183 and 190 present phased detailed studies of forty-three hectares of Britsh Rail land designated for redevelopment, including the existing main-line station at Stratford East, London E15. Political, social and economic options required consideration, occasioning phased future development. As Paul Finch writes, "For Price this means the sort of problem he loves: not so much a building , more the creation of a network of facilities and information..." – to relocate the main station, shifting it west over the North London Line directly engaging the North London Line, the Docklands Light Railway, London Transport's Central Line and the British Rail main line. The station is then double-sided with access from both North and South. The success of any project here is founded on the co-operation of all the transport networks converging on this site.

Privatization of the rail network creates an insurmountable impass between client and architect, and the fate of the scheme is ultimately affected by the approval of the Jubilee Line Extension.

Sir Bob Reid, then chairman of British Rail and Bernard Gambrill of British Rail must be acknowledged for their continued support for the work of CPA throughout these projects.

Projects 216 APPEX, 205 RINK, 195 CONTROL and 192 NEWLINK relate to aspects of research for the briefs 183/190 and look beyond the site to a future development of the Thames Gateway and Channel Tunnel Rail link.

The approach to the Stratford design is summed up in five points: 1.The greatest sign of honesty of service is the Station Clock. 2. Transportation is about the quality and condition in which one arrives at one's own or some other's front door. Station, airports, bus stations and ports are merely necessary punctuation spots. 3. Stratford is an ever-changing amalgam of different modes of transport – the station should provide a Battenburg cake of a complex, an appetisingly protected range of choice. 4. Good railway architecture must be seen as that where the long-term aims do not distort frequency of beneficial short-term growth and change. The former should not encourage one-off expensive follies, nor the latter be seen as an excuse for cost-cutting and the second-rate. 5. Not for stations the futile panacea for delay of designer lounges and cheap booze stores.

Some additional notes:

The people – they are the super critics of a piece of architecture but only at 5.30pm when they are late. This relates to all architecture but is highlighted with networks and systems of movement and transportation – the change from interest to attention.

Access, service and interchange facilities for passengers must encompass all the available choices for transportation in order to enable the Station to respond to changing demands in short, medium and long terms.The present deplorable standard of passenger facilities found at Stratford should be replaced or improved by introducing equipment, services and products that can either be re-used in the new Station or at least serve as "test-beds". Such items should be readily recognized and seen to be part of a process of improvement rather than merely the tinkering with the old. Introduction of transportable if not mobile units should be encouraged.

Absence of WCs makes refreshment and waiting a hazardous occupation on platform 6/8.

Automatic vending (of tickets) has been discounted – "non desirable, due to exceptional vandalism" – Is vandalism due to any or all of: - location, equipment, supervision?

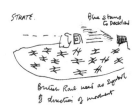

ref. Paul Finch, "Anticipating the unexpected", BD, 17 June 1988.

Opposite:
078. Watercolour of view looking towards new entrance and concourse of Stratford East Station.

i want it built
of nothing &
yet to occupy.

BR 25618/8

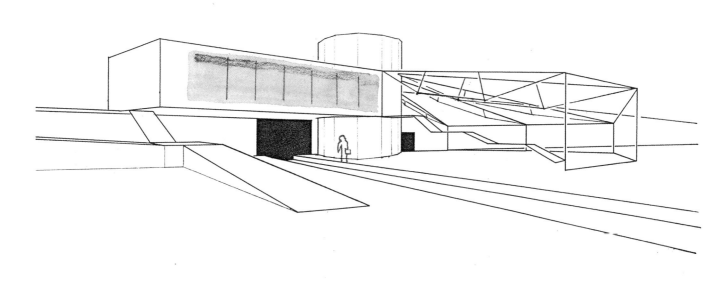

078

i want it built
of nothing &
yet to occupy.

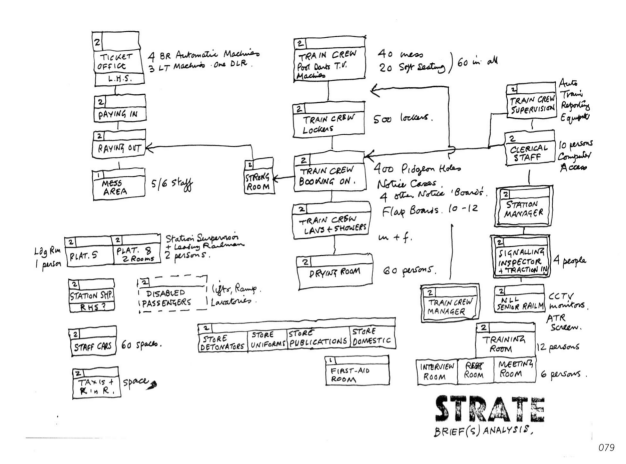

STRATE

BRIEF(S) ANALYSIS.

079

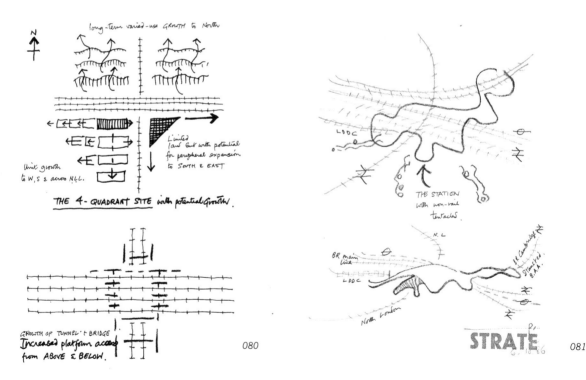

THE 4-QUADRANT SITE with potential Growth.

GROWTH OF TUNNEL + BRIDGE
Increased platform access from ABOVE & BELOW.

080

STRATE

081

This page:

079. organisational diagram of station activities and utilities.

080. the 4-quadrant site.

081. linking of networks.

Opposite:

082. section through station.

083. alteration of station concourse showing positioning bow-string
arch in relation to walkway.

084. detail of steel castings for bow-string arch.

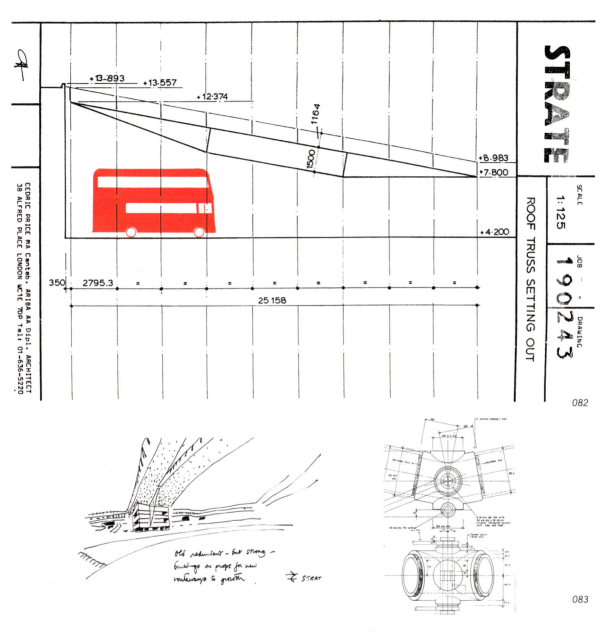

082

083

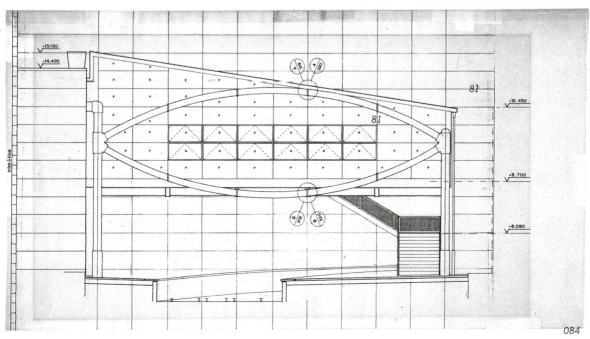

084

205
RINK

RIVER THAMES

GRAVESEND
(MB & CP)

SHORNE CP

A
VERY
'DELIC
ARE

*Milton Chantry,
Gravesend*
KENT

Until the nineteenth century Milton was
quite separate from the port of Gravesend

as were a number of smaller buildings.) Fi
can be had across the Thames to Gravesend
New Tavern Fort by *Milton Chantry.* Parth

Tilbury Fort

205 27 RINK

CEDRIC PRICE MA Cantab. ARIBA AA Dipl. ARCHIT
68 ALFRED PLACE LONDON WC1E 7DP Tel: 01-636

CORRIDOR

CONTENTS?

Canterbury Way
QE2 Bridge

VISUALLY INTENSE
SEGMENT

River Thames

85. Investigations of Thames Gateway area - collage

CEDRIC PRICE MA Cantab. ARIBA AA Dipl. ARCHI
68 ALFRED PLACE LONDON WC1E 7DP Tel: 01-63

RINK

205 26

JOHN LYALL

—

John Lyall is an architect and Managing Director of John Lyall Architects. Lyall worked as a recent graduate in the offices of Cedric Price Architects in the 1970s. In 2000 he was the RIBA Vice President for Future Studies and is current chair of their Education Validation Taskforce.

Constant movement –
Cedric Price and education.

For an architect who has often eschewed the role of being a regular design tutor, Cedric Price is a naturally good teacher, a challenging critic, and someone who thinks profoundly about the future of architectural education, and has done so since the 1960s.

The training of young architects has received the same degree of strategic, lateral thinking as any of Price's projects. The starting point for such strategies is the defining expectation of what future architects will be capable of. Far more meaningful than throwing up attractive award-winning buildings is an evolving responsibility to help society change with or without technology. In this respect, in Price's world, the architect takes on many roles with many talents so that it is counter-productive for each architect to have the same education.

One of the earliest and best examples of this approach was formulated in May 1966 (a week when the Rolling Stones' 'Paint it Black' was No.1 in the British pop charts and the first unmanned spacecraft had just landed on the moon). It was published in the *Architect's Journal* under the title of *The National School Plan*[1].

The proposals are:

A. All schools of architecture in the UK should be co-ordinated to produce a range of architectural educational investigations far more comprehensive than that now offered by any single school.

B. Students should be enabled to move from one school to another during the average five year full – time course.

C. The value of such movement would lie in the advantage gained by the student from the particular quality of any one school at any one time. The particular quality must be clear in the content of the school's curriculum.

D. The particular quality of a school would be enabled to develop far beyond present possibilities through an established and agreed exchange and joint usage of primary information and instruction. A Joint Schools Commission (JSC) would be established to prepare and administer such programming. It would offer full and part-time employment as at present offered by individual schools.

E. The uniqueness of any school should be accompanied in every case by the shared courses, and such shared courses would primarily be determined by the advantage to be gained from mass participation.

F. There would be realistic acceptance of the shortage of ideal staff and money would be spent, not in hiring second-rate replicas, but in enabling as many students as possible to come in contact with the good ones.

G. The possibility of development of the unique qualities of individual schools would require an increase in student mobility (see B) and at the same time permit concentration and reinforcement of particular staff at any one school.

In the small, dense print of the (then) stuffy *AJ*, Price's radical, but always sensible, ideas did not receive the exposure they deserved. However, his article was run coincidentally only a few pages after a long-winded report about a conference of the University Heads of Schools. It was a useful reminder of how painfully slow any real changes happened in architectural education (then, as now!), and that according to the conference certain schools, the Bartlett (University College London) in particular, were considered to be more "experimental" than others in the sixties. However, in his National Schools Plan discourse, Price comments:

Schools are becoming increasingly nervous of experiment and, in some cases, are using 'technology' not as a springboard but more as an unchanging cornerstone on which to base some form of bastard classic education pattern. On the other hand the profession, groggy with the attention being paid to it, is totally directionless and prey to the short-term overtures of a derelict building industry.

Thus it is proposed that a fuller awareness of the state of the businessis beneficial for a school since it is in this formative period that the embryo architect is best equipped and serviced to take a long, slow first look at things and start to order priorities to his own satisfaction. The school must provide an ordered framework in which varied directions of architectural development are put to exacting tests.

The real issue was that all schools generally adopted the same methodology and had the same outputs. There seemed to be an inevitable homogeneity of purpose for all the UK's graduate architects to come out with the same skills and outlook. They would then fit nicely into a profession that knew exactly what it wanted.

In spite of the newer, confident-looking post war architecture resulting from socially driven building programmes and the Festival of Britain (1952), architectural practice in the UK was about providing a 'service' and fulfilling a 'need'. The exciting and busy period for architects in the 1950s and 60s left them little time to think about real social futures and possibility of the architect's role changing from the traditional pre-war model. The arrival on the scene of an individual like Cedric Price and a group like Archigram[2] must have been a breath of fresh air to students and young architects, and a damned irritation to established academics and practitioners who had previously felt in control and unassailable.

*It has been assumed that the immediate demands made by one of the most archaic industries, **building** (translated into gentlemanly terms by the Royal Institute of British Architects and pipelined through to the schools by the Board of Architectural Education), are a direct concern of embryo architects, but also, and more important, that as the industry as it is constituted today is the rightful heir to the attentions of architects of the future – that five years ahead is the future in relation to healthy progressive artifactual endeavours.*

Similarly, while the trials and difficulties encountered by the profession today require to be overcome, the solutions adopted, often through expediency, require careful scrutiny before being translated into educational theory. Also, there is something extremely unhealthy in the 'holier than thou' professional grafting demands

of the RIBA on the public and private patronage at large. Society does not owe architects a living and not necessarily attention either. Finally, too close to a liaison – often for urgent, if not admirable reasons – between a group of the profession, a branch of the building industry and a collective of clients can result in particular 'band aid' solutions being reinforced ad absurdum (an example of this is the contrived, even if ingenious, uses being discovered for the CLASP System[3]).

Price's work was influencing a small, but growing number of architects who were also teaching. His time-based urban projects undoubtedly affected the more stylised, but similarly optimistic outpourings of Archigram. By the late sixties and early seventies, the strategy-based and process-based work was beginning to take hold in the UK schools because of the direct influence of Price and teachers who were taken by his work. Occasionally Price would appear to run a workshop, give a lecture or sparkle at a crit that was exciting, unforgettable and transforming for students. As a student myself at the Architectural Association in the 1970s, I was encouraged to believe that everything I designed was a political act and that there was great joyful optimism that the world would change, that it was changing now and that we had all better keep up!

It was inevitable then that Price's *National Schools Plan* should be conceived rather like one of his urban strategy projects – logical and uncompromising in its design for future adaptation or obsolescence.

One of the main premises behind the plan was that no student need have the same education as another. The education would not necessarily be based at one institution but the student would be free to travel the country between teachers and schools and to configure the creative learning that suits him or her. This would produce a cohort of graduates with a wide range of skills but still under the umbrella of 'architecture'.

Useful education feedback is talked of, but in general the most likely effect of such a move is to increase the tail's capacity to wag the dog. It is considered extremely unlikely that a single standard five-year course can ever be the ideal preparation for a variety of specialisations. The five-year period can be cut and specialisation take place earlier (as at the Bartlett School of Architecture), but even this is considered a 'band-aid' action since there is still a marked division of intent implied in the midway changeover. The dog and tail situation should be eliminated and at any one school a totally co-ordinated curriculum evolved for four to five years.

Cedric Price's *National Schools Plan* is still relevant and still necessary more than 36 years later. There is more student mobility now in terms of foreign exchange and the growing trend for changing schools after the first three years in education. The American system of earning 'credits' and pacing the duration of one's education to suit the individual (and becoming more accepted in the UK) is also echoed in the Plan. But the constantly interactive bubbling firmament of architectural education that I think that Price envisaged would never be permitted on a national scale. Would it not be too uncontrollable and unpredictable for the government and universities to encourage? On close examination the only real headaches would be those of administration forty years on. In today's world of cash-strapped higher education and acute student poverty, the sheer economics of the Price *Plan* is tempting. The overall quality of education received is raised by allowing all students access to the best teachers.

It is useful to note that the *National Schools Plan* was conceived at about the same time as Price's POTTERIES THINKBELT which proposed a system of higher education based on unlimited student mobility via the external rail networks. Study of it gives an interesting physical framework for the Plan.

By 1970 Price's demands for change continued but the tone was even more direct. As students we particularly enjoyed and were encouraged by the 'Cedric Price Column' in *Archigram Nine* magazine[4]. *The major justification for the existence of any form of advanced voluntary organised education should be that it enables its users TO DISTORT TIME AND LOCATION IN THE LEARNING PROCESS. Whilst students are at present one of the most mobile social groups of technologically advanced societies, the nature of their own particular production plants – schools, colleges and universities, is static, intro spective, parochial, inflexible and not very useful. Architectural students suffer from this rotten servicing system as much as anyone. The result – apparent in every school of architecture – is boredom and/or discontent of students and staff alike; lack of conviction follows. In fact the maintenance of the staff/student concept in architectural education is one of the major causes of its accelerating impotence.*

Definitions for PSEUDS:

1. Those who pay to learn other people's mistakes are called STUDENTS.

2. Those who are paid to learn by their own mistakes are called PRACTITIONERS.

3. Those who imagine that the repetition of mistakes in an ordered well-defined way is intellectually beneficial are called TEACHERS.

There is no reason to suppose that it is best to receive between the ages of 17 and 25 and to dispense at any time beyond that age. The receiving/ dispensing equation is one which should never be written. CLASSIFICATION OF PEOPLE RELATED TO PARTICULAR OPERATIONAL MENTAL PATTERNING IS FALSE. However, it is bloody convenient for lazy administrators and cowardly academics.

U.K.1970. 6,000 architectural students with an expensive 4/5 – year ticket to work – waste. 10+ schools of architecture showing signs of advanced decay. The remainder of schools concealing such signs. If learning value distortion of time and location is to be realised in time, then we must move FAST – all of us – on feet, by phone, tape, film ESP, with credit cards, coins on a string, other people's birds or fellows – even local authority money.

JOKE - Q – If a single student occupies 9 sq. metres of static school space for five days a week, what has he lost? A - £200+ per year travel money – spent on rental of that dust covered drawing board space.

By MOVING to a better scene we not only show constructive discontent but reinforce the value of our chosen node. Even some existing schools of architecture could become useful, uneven, unbalanced work centres for people in a hurry. A dynamic control problem for the administrators is created. No longer can they ask – 'how many students for how long?' Rather they must budget for the continuous servicing of nomadic activists – of all ages. HIT THE ROAD – FOR A 50 – YEAR JOURNEY.

Imagine *The National Schools Plan* now and how it would work today. It was written before the availability of fax machines and predates the World Wide Web. Now you can plug in your laptop on the train – mobile learning is a reality. On the whole British schools of architecture are excellent and thankfully each one maintains its individual character, in spite of an all-pervading need to control output by the Architects Registration Board. This 'control' destroys precisely what lies at the heart of *The National Schools Plan*, making it all the more important for architects and educators to be reminded of it: freedom, choice and self-regulation, all leading to greater creativity and diversity.

'How would Cedric Price have tackled this?' is a question that I know many people who have encountered him personally or through the work, ask themselves – some of them currently heads of schools and practices in the UK and abroad. With any scheme, whether at college or in practice, it is worth asking the same question – now and in the future.

JUDE KELLY

___

Jude Kelly recently left the West Yorkshire Playhouse (arguably the most dynamic and successful provincial theatre in the UK) after 12 years as Artistic Director and Chief Executive. Kelly began her theatrical career in Leicester in 1975 as an actress. She became artistic director of Solent People's Theatre in 1976, and in the 1980s established an international reputation for Battersea Arts Centre as its artistic director. She has worked at the National Theatre of Brent, the Bristol Old Vic and the Lyric Hammersmith. Kelly was awarded the OBE for her services to the theatre in 1997. In 2003 she received a Fellowship Award from the National Endowment for Science, Technology and the Arts (NESTA) to pursue greater freedom of creative expression. She is developing the METAL studio in West Hampstead, London as a centre for all artists to experiment, collaborate and share research.

In the mood for the future.

Cedric Price – a giant capacity for vision and the generosity to share it. Cedric Price – an inspiration and an influence to me before I even knew of him.

Inspiration One: INTER-ACTION.

I was a drama student and a young theatre director in the 1970s. There were three spaces in London at the time that epitomised this era of freethinking and challenge, the Roundhouse, the Institute of Contemporary Art (ICA) and INTER-ACTION.

The Roundhouse in Camden, north London was a converted railway goods yard – a round brick building where horses turned the carriages around. It converted joyfully into a place for 'happenings', rock gigs, circus-style shows and radical epic theatre. Camden High Street was then the Mecca for hippie merchandise and generalised alternative life style, matching perfectly with its exciting, anarchic venue where individual freedom was inevitable since the space was too cavernous to ever feel architecturally 'navigated'. The clientele and this physical randomness gave visitors to the Roundhouse a permanent sense of party; full of students, ex-students, drop-outs, lecturers, radical rock musicians and fringe performers. It was politically unfocused and generally accommodating of all things liberal. Dress code: alternative.

By contrast the ICA, first located in Dover Street and now in its present home on The Mall between Buckingham Palace and Downing Street, housed a sophisticated discourse on current cultural values through avant-garde exhibitions, film, debate and performance. The aristocratic environment played well with the rarefied air of intellectual exchange and hard-core Modernism, made all the more important by its elegant surroundings and proximity to the heart of the establishment. Cool and competitive, it enjoyed creating the new elite of opinion formers. Dress code: designer trendy.

INTER-ACTION sat in the middle of a council estate in Kentish Town. The artistic director, Ed Berman, entrepreneur, showman and social philosopher, stimulated huge debate on the purpose of art and creativity, who was included or excluded by current attitudes and how the arts could effect practical and political change and challenge expectation. Inter-Action's aim was on the one hand to create a partnership between a low-income, poorly educated community and on the other, artists and political activists. It also aimed to radicalise conventional arts audience boundries and give art and artists a special, key role in the expression of community aspiration. Cedric Price's building was both a symbol of the future and a method of working out how to move towards it. The building was a low-rise collection of geometric possibilities in steel. It was new, properly heated, had large windows, was surrounded by greenery and sat next to flats, houses and a railway line. Everything about its assembly could change to accommodate a limitless set of ideas, some unknown, some emerging, some unrealisable at this early stage. It was untainted by nost-algia, historical reference or reverence. It suggested a practical realism. It belonged only to NOW.

I remember the building feeling at ease with its local, under-nourished neighbourhood despite its own state of the art energy. It neither patronised nor compromised and its flexibility provided a creative input of its own. It made grand ideas seem possible and gave small ideas grace.

Inspiration Two: FUN PALACE.

In 1999 I was invited to see inside the Millennium Dome, empty of its future content and empty too of any philosophy necessary to inspire or strengthen a commitment to a better future. As it gradually filled up with gadgets, food franchises and low-grade controversy, I reflected on the dream hatched by theatre director, Joan Littlewood and Cedric Price of the FUN PALACE; their definition of FUN: "seeking the unfamiliar and ultimately transcending it".

Arrive and leave by train, bus, mono-rail, hovercraft, tube, car or on foot at any time you want to – or just have a look at it as you pass. The information screens will show you what's happening. No need to look for an entrance – just walk in anywhere. No doors, foyers, queues or commissionaires. Look around, take a lift, a ramp, an escalator... If it's too wet, the roof will stop the rain but not the light... We are building, a short term plaything in which all of us can realise the possibilities and delights that the 20th century environment owes us. It must last no longer than we need it.
Joan Littlewood and Cedric Price, 1963[1].

Their idea should have influenced a project like the Dome. But she an artist, he an architect, both prepared to stand or fall by their beliefs and ready to sink their teeth into the less courageous. Not the sort of people that politicians want to have around when hatching compromises like the Dome. The next time that two great, thinking figures offer us such vistas – will we participate? Will we lobby? Or will we wait and see what the politicians do and then speak of our impotence and disappointment? Everyone relished condemning the Dome – but would those same newspaper editors have backed whole-heartedly an artist-led scheme instead? Any radical grapple with the social, environmental, economic and artistic status quo has to suffer the indignities of derision, mainly due to our fear of change.

Price more recently had an exhibition at the Canadian Centre of Architecture called *Mean Time* (MEAN), exploring the relationships between time, movement and space and its influence on the built environment. When I saw the title, I thought of NOW. Maybe to achieve the mix of risk, love, science and serendipity proposed by the FUN PALACE, we need to make *Generous Time* and let artists have their head.

Inspiration Three: METAL.

"Divide the space with light", said Cedric. I was showing him my idea – an artistic laboratory space that I had called METAL. Built in 1912, it was the original ticket office for West Hampstead Station and subsequently served as a metal working shop for fifty years until, semi-derelict and forlorn it beckoned for some attention. By this time I had met Cedric. Had good conversations with him – always encouraging and challenging and always funny.

I had asked Cedric to view my project at an early stage. The endless downpour of rain and unremitting black sky on that day seemed impertinent to his beautifully laundered shirt, 'Groucho' cigar and unathletic torso. Watching him wandering through the old brick building I observed his imagination at work: the practical side considered drainage, roof repair, subsidence from train disturbance, fore-exits, sound-proofing, load-bearing capacity and so on – expert, incisive and exhaustive. At the same time he questioned how the building could be "released". He asked lots and lots of questions about its use, particularly about its emotional one, its moral one. What place did this building have in my life? What need did it fulfil? Why did I want to engage with my space? What life, companionship, style of artistic relationships did I want? How do I perceive light and space in different artistic activities? Was it a new energetic vision or simply a diversion from other more "real" tasks that I should be addressing about my life? Did he ask all his clients these questions, I asked? "Yes, otherwise I don't want them as clients."

Cedric went on to explain that so often architects are asked to design buildings for clients that are using the excitement of the project to replace emptiness elsewhere. He was clearly only interested in projects devised for genuine creative reasons –

otherwise he said, "it's a waste of landscape and my time."

Cedric is a formidable philosopher for values and shared responsibility. He is a teacher of thinking. He helped me to acknowledge that artistic subtleties and human dynamic need to be taken into account. He then gave me a task. Initially, like so many of Cedric's suggestions, it seemed simple, but on reflection became a life-changing exercise. "Draw up a list" he said, "of what you know and believe you should be doing and itemise them down the side of the page. Create a time line at the bottom of when you have to complete your goals. Then select three thickness' of line – thin lines for the least important tasks, medium thickness for tasks that don't have too much relevance, thick lines for tasks that are crucial to your life. Fill in how you are doing so far.

Most people complete the thin lines first because they are easy, the thick ones left until later because they need "proper time". As a result the fundamental issues are put off – often forever and the project goes ahead without the most important ideas in place. There is no distinction between a Price building project and a life – the client is the project and the building is part of that. The question becomes, "Is the building helping you to further your life and fulfil 'thick tasks' or creating new short term 'thin tasks' which serve as an illusory activity or purpose?" Price is dead against creating buildings as a displacement activity.

Use time well.
Use time creatively.
Don't trap time.
Don't let time slip away.
Don't be scared.
Be brave.

SIMON ALLFORD

—

Simon Allford is an architect and principal partner in Allford Hall Monighan Morris

On Price and Value –
Constructing the Idea.

I have known Cedric for all my forty odd years. For twenty years he was a family friend who engaged my sisters and I, together and separately, in various conversations and events: a cricket match; a debate on the relative merits of Sheffield Wednesday and Stoke; the design of torpedoes manufactured from a plentiful supply of Havana cigar tubes; a trip in a white limousine to see the film *The Great Gatsby*. We knew he was an architect who had designed the Snowdon AVIARY with Frank Newby – because we often visited it.

For the last twenty years he has remained a friend and he is of course still an architect. He has changed, as have we. We still engage, but in different ways in different conversations. Now we will meet and talk over breakfast or lunch about what was, or is going on in life – he spoke with a smile at my eldest sister's memorial service – and of course architecture.

Much is made of the special role Cedric has in architecture, the particular view he has made his own. His love of paradox and his delight in constructing the idea not the building; his interest in the user ahead of the architecture; his preference for the individual rather than the organisation. I however have a different perception of the office of Cedric Price Architects. For Cedric has spent most of these forty years inventing a particular model office. Not the same as any other but nevertheless a model for many.

The office was until recently located not in a virtual site but a 19th century Central London 'chambers' in Alfred Place. The presence of the office nevertheless was felt well beyond its strategic site. It was elegantly if discreetly signed, it had two floors of desks and a reception and a place of reflection at high level – the White Room. It had a very special modus operandi – working hours from 8:00 to 3:30 to ensure that a large part of the day remained free for all to pursue other projects and interests. The staff were encouraged to stay for one or two years, rarely longer sometimes shorter. There were a series of particular pre-planned events for the office each year. Once a year those who had left would return for a party. The office was well managed and all information was carefully presented and documented utilising a system of bespoke rubber stamps.

Projects that entered the office were subjected to a rigorous examination and selection process – Inception and Feasibility – assessing their value to the office; the potential within them for enquiry; and the opportunity to utilise them in speculations on improving the human condition. Different analytical techniques were employed – diagrams, notes, drawings, text, conversation, models and importantly, inventive titles. All were presented without fuss and with the necessary economy – the underlying aim was to communicate the office's perception of the practical value of the project. This way a decision could be made.

Those projects which passed this test, entered the Scheme Design Stage. The client and their brief – if indeed either existed, for a number of these projects were speculations that might invent future clients – were always questioned. The POTTERIES THINKBELT[1] was not only a brilliant and prescient proposition for education as urban regenerator but offered a vision which was both a critique of and counter to the contemporary pre-occupation with new out of town campus universities. Anyway, it was accepted that all projects had many clients, so the exploration of the core components of the brief was vital. In particular there was a preoccupation with time and measurement and their impact on possible use. If the project manifested itself as requiring a building then the architecture of this building would be considered as the product of the analysis. The potentially barren outcome of this programmatic system of operations was rigorously countered by a clear view that in form and detail the project must offer delight to those who built, utilised and eventually demolished it. Projects anticipated their own redundancy.

Once proven to be of interest, the project would then move into the Production Information Stage. This would take a specific form precisely tailored to the anticipated Procurement Stage. The way information was presented was economic and appropriate – it was always clear and well defined and designed in response to the time allocated. For each project, the expenditure of effort was carefully valued. The package as assembled would communicate what was to be built and when, what was important to the office and what it would leave to the different skills of other consultants and fabricators, operators and users. Information was as prescriptive as the Feasibility had suggested it needed to be – and no more. While a user manual might be required, it would always support the view the office held that any project recognised and defined the limits of the architect's control.

Indeed the desire to delay, wherever possible, premature decision making, reflected the view that unnecessary control of the building's construction and use would only hamper the emergence of the 'unimagined uses' for the project. It was believed that, in both design and occupation, these would be invented or discovered by others. This idea was given focus, but deliberately not definitive form in the Inter-Action Centre. The office commitment to demolition was recently confirmed by Cedric's rejection of the idea of a possible listing. Doubt was as important to the design process as demolition was to the construction process. Once the Production Stage was complete, the project went into the Tender Stage. This stage took many different forms and indeed it would be brought forward if the initial analysis suggested that a number of the earlier stages were not required and the project could be 'fast tracked'.

Sometimes this stage was missed out altogether and collaboration with a constructor was preferred. If a tender was pursued, it might be issued to a selected number of contractors – not all of the traditional building variety. The office had a keen interest in transferring and adopting technologies from other industries. Alternatively it might take the form of an exhibition, publication, lecture or conversation. In all cases the focus was most specifically and without exception on the tendering of ideas.

As a result of the earlier decisions the Construction Phase was unique to each project. Operations on site were responsive to the prior enquiries into economy and the benefits of prototypes were appreciated. The sites were very different including not only Blackpool, Regents Park, The Potteries, Kentish Town, East London and Paris but also reports on Air Structures and Steel Housing – all were 'sites' where the idea was 'constructed'. A building's anticipated lifespan was a key consideration and it impacted on the failure and success of a number of details, as did the experience or not of the assistants. Aspirations and technology were not always matched – but it was acknowledged that if virtuoso techno-logical wit was required, it was likely that the wrong questions had been asked.

Anyway buildings were often not the answer – this view was always evident in the work of the office. Undoubtedly the most important oper-ation of the office was in the 'construction of the idea'. Not necessarily on site or on paper but in the minds of all those who became aware of the work. As was recently pointed out to me the timber clad Blackpool Restaurant with its' 'plimsole line' of glazing was source material for one of our own projects. My understanding of this office as a model for practice is probably different to anyone else's. This is my construct of how it operated and what it did – it is based on my experiences, various conversations and my exploration of many projects. It is the model for an office that I have been inspired to pursue.

So you may ask, is it real? It is as real as any of the projects – regardless of whether they have or have not been built, they have all been 'constructed'. An office, like any project, exists in the mind of the observer as much as it does in any reality. As Cedric himself put it, in reference to the annual Royal Agricultural Show at Stoneleigh – any place is as real as your experience of it. Of course now that I have finally constructed this model office in my head Cedric has constructed a new office – based in carefully selected venues in and around Marylebone. As always with Cedric, a new model is emerging.

6 – REJUVENATION & RETHINK

ALLOWANCE FOR CONSTRUCTIVE CHANGE AND REMOVAL OF INAPPROPRIATE CLUTTER

247 METAL	X27 WALSALL	230 HALMAG	226 GATARD	220 MAGNET	222 TASKFORCE

"SPACE AS SPEED IN TIME"

SOCIAL CONVENIENCE
HABIT
SOCIAL RETHINK
SOCIAL CHANGE & PERMANENCE
CONVENIENCE THROUGH REPETITION
SAFETY
HABIT THROUGH USAGE
HABIT THROUGH LEARNING
PRODUCTION - MAKING THINGS
IMPROVEMENT - THROUGH PRODUCTION

6 –
REJUVENATION AND RETHINK

222
TASKFORCE

Seven volunteer students from the diploma school of the Architectural Association School of Architecture, London signed a 'Taskforce' contract for a year's programme. The contract, outlined by Price but completed by each student, defined what it was that he/she wanted to achieve in the year, how it would be achieved and how it would be assessed. All students passed and received their diploma.

Ref: "The Real Issues", BD, 16 July 1982
Ref: "The World About US - Cedric Price on Schools", BD, 16 July 1982.

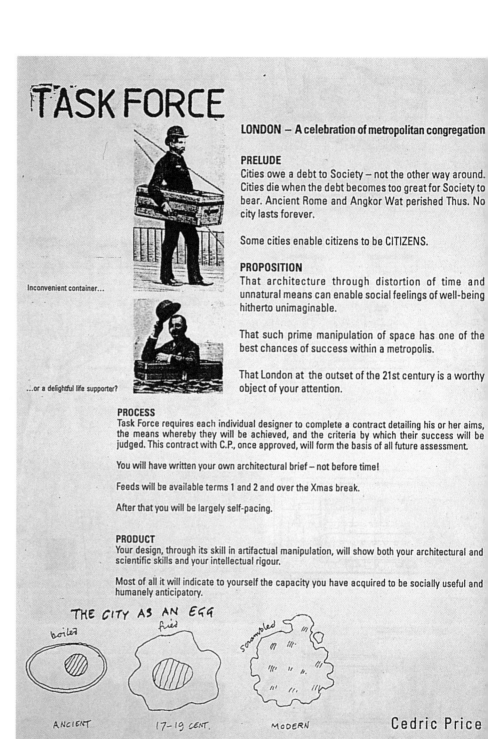

TASK FORCE

Inconvenient container...

...or a delightful life supporter?

LONDON – A celebration of metropolitan congregation

PRELUDE
Cities owe a debt to Society – not the other way around. Cities die when the debt becomes too great for Society to bear. Ancient Rome and Angkor Wat perished Thus. No city lasts forever.

Some cities enable citizens to be CITIZENS.

PROPOSITION
That architecture through distortion of time and unnatural means can enable social feelings of well-being hitherto unimaginable.

That such prime manipulation of space has one of the best chances of success within a metropolis.

That London at the outset of the 21st century is a worthy object of your attention.

PROCESS
Task Force requires each individual designer to complete a contract detailing his or her aims, the means whereby they will be achieved, and the criteria by which their success will be judged. This contract with C.P., once approved, will form the basis of all future assessment.

You will have written your own architectural brief – not before time!

Feeds will be available terms 1 and 2 and over the Xmas break.

After that you will be largely self-pacing.

PRODUCT
Your design, through its skill in artifactual manipulation, will show both your architectural and scientific skills and your intellectual rigour.

Most of all it will indicate to yourself the capacity you have acquired to be socially useful and humanely anticipatory.

THE CITY AS AN EGG

boiled

fried

scrambled

ANCIENT

17-19 CENT.

MODERN

Cedric Price

"Educational refreshment...
five years of distorted adulthood are really best spent looking at that which has not been considered before, rather than refining that which has."
Dimensions, BD, 23 July 1993.

086. poster page launching the brief for the year's programme.

- Conceit
- Pretence
- Dreams
- Untruths

THE STATIC
'public' exchange   Self-pace observation

Secret gardens - and conversation
THE MOBILE

public choice of observation

The City is not merely a toy for the well-serviced individual.

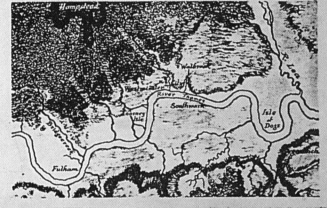

History of place – not nostalgia of moment.

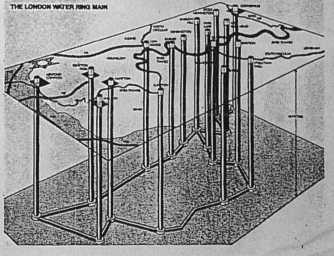

Infra-structures do not 'just sprout fancy nozzles'.
(Buckminster Fuller)

226
GATARD

The conversion of a pigsty (which was no longer used for its original purpose) into residential space and workshops. The project is complete and has been sold on to accommodate rural industries.

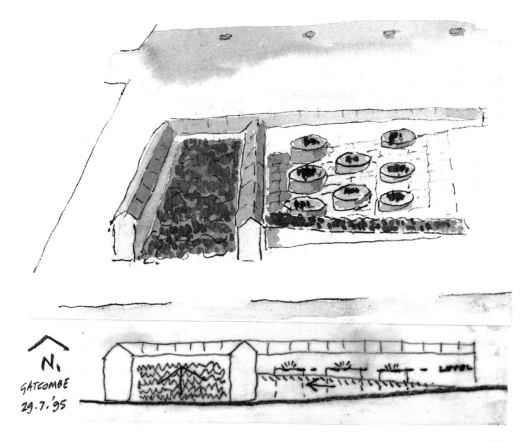

087

087. watercolour overview of site with new planting and section showing change in levels.

247
METAL

The brief, written by CPA for the client, theatre director Jude Kelly in response to an initial site visit. Kelly's request to CPA is to view an existing building, the former station offices for West Hampstead Station, as a place for artists to develop new work unhindered by administrative/institutional overheads.

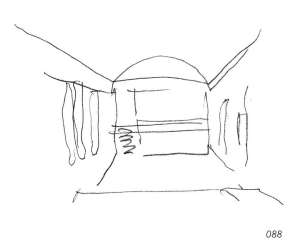

088

METAL: AN AMALGAM OF THE ACTION OF DOING, COMBINED WITH THE MANUFACTURING PROCESS DETERMINED BY TIME.

- THE MAKING OF AN OBJECT
- PAINTING A PAINTING
- ENGINEERING, A HYDROLOGICAL EXPERIMENT
- DESIGN EXERCISE : ASSEMBLING A PIECE OF CLOTHING

ALL RESULT IN AN ADDITIVE PROCESS COMBINING A CONGLOMERATE OF THE SUM TOTAL IN TIME, BEING A PROCESS DESCRIBED IN TIME AS A CONTINUOUS PROCEDURE.

THE ART IS PROCEDURE, THE PRODUCT   IS OBSERVATION OF THE SATISFACTION TO ALL THE OPERATIVES; IN CONTRAST (FOR EXAMPLE) TO THE 'SHEEP' – THE AUDIENCE – ASSEMBLED (AT THEIR OWN COST AND IN THEIR OWN TIME) AT THE TATE MODERN.

Cedric price 20·1·02

The museum is a house - or at least - a nano place.
088. interior view of METAL.

220
MAGNET

Magnets are applied to 10 sites in the Greater London area. Feasibility studies have also been carried out in comparable locations in Tokyo.

Project assistant, Keiichi Saiki.

"It is quite possible for the world as we know it now to become unregulable in important fields in that it might pass the point beyond which any considered action might have a statistical probablity of being worse than random. There are many situations in which to be systematically late is to be systematically wrong."

Sir Geoffrey Vickers, Value Systems & Social Progress, 1908.

"Unsocial Services. Well into our self-financing MAGNET project,the Office is reviewing the first answers we received from Central and Local Government Officials – the questin being the likely, rather than desirable range of future UK Social Services. So far, Central Government did not speculate but merely predicted more or less of the same; Local Government was far more useful, imaginative and constructive. Perhaps it is to be expected – the former being embarrassed by the absence of any long plans by HMG and fearing private specualtion being mistaken for 'a government leak', while the latter suspecting no central plans, hopes for a future of whatever form."

*Price Probes, **BD**, 13 Jan. 1995.*

*Ref: "Magnetism Personified", **BD**, 24 May 1996.*

Anticipatory Architecture is essential to equate its use and delight with contemporary social, economic and political items of the new. Thus, Anticipatory Architecture must only anticipate the nature and form of future humane services that require architectural attention for them to function but also design future enclosures that through their siting, form, life span and uniqueness enable activities hitherto impossible and therefore socially undefined. Community and certainty, solitude and doubt must be welcomed equally.

An excerpt from the catalogue accompanying an exhibition of MAGNET at the Architecture Foundation describes the project:

A series of short life structures, to be funded by local authorities or civic bodies, which would be used to set up new kinds of public amenity and public movement. They would occupy spaces not usually seen as sites available to the public such as the air space above roads, streets, parks, lakes and railways. Magnets are designed to generate new kinds of access, views, sanctuary, safety, information and delight. They might help you cross a road in a range of ways, with lifts, escalators and stairs allowing for differences in level of mobility. Magnets can provide, for example, library facilities or better access to a railway station and simultaneously give you the sorts of view for which you are normally expected to pay. They are designed to "overload" underused or misused sites, to make them more delightful and better fun.

Magnets are deliberately mobile, adaptable and re-usable,so that they do not become, as often happens with buildings, inactive, inflexible, institutionalized, formalized, privatized or redundant. The structures, or "tools" which make up Magnets are inherently mobile: cranes,airport transporters, scissor lifts - so they can be hired for the length of time needed and adjusted or moved elsewhere as required. Magnets are both pragmatic and polemic in the way they turn space to the public advantage. They are not an end in themselves but encourage the continual necessity for change.

089. MAGNET - early sketch.
090. MAGNET - statement, CP.
091, 092. templates devised by CPA to generate speed and distance diagram.
093. speed and distance diagram.

089

MAGNET

MAGNETS are installed on existing metropolitan sites which are at present UNDERUSED or MISUSED.

Their SITING enriches the intensity of the city grain.

The STRUCTURES act as both INSERTS AND TRANSPLANTS providing socially beneficial movement routes. Their PLANNING encourages adjacent future growth while the FIXED-LIFE structures enable VARIATION & RE-ASSEMBLY to be undertaken with speed and minimal disruption.

To establish a valid equation between contemporary social aspirations and Architecture, it is essential to add to the latter Doubt, Delight and Change as design criteria.

MAGNETS are an example of the necessity of Anticipatory Design.

Cedric Price 15. 3. '96

090

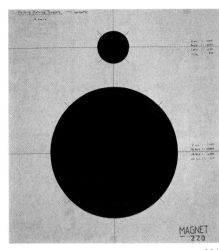

091

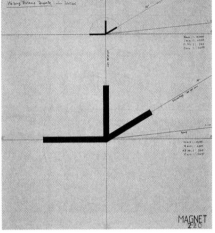

092

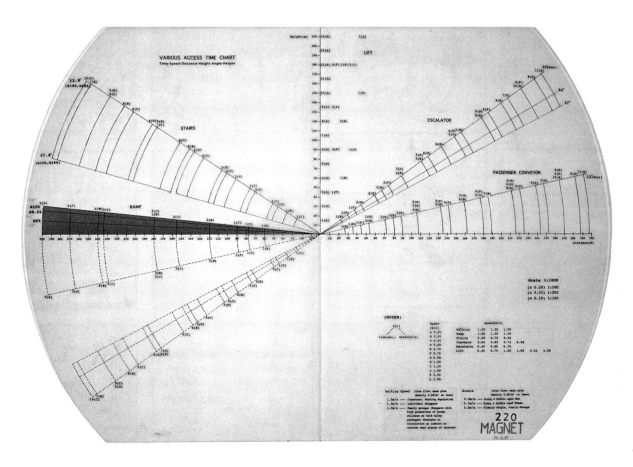

093

1

Temporary protection
Length of linker — STEPS, STAIRS,
— short-hand LIFT —

Size of platforms — Resting AREA
Observation AREA

Ease of access — Hanging around
Ease of change of level Space - safely.
Threshold safety — NOT MUCH ground level
Congregation

STAIRWAYS

094a

2

Ease of access
VIEWING & ENJOYING
Safety.
Ref. to small information

PROMENADE

094b

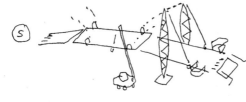

3

Platform OBSERVATION - with SAFETY
Cross-routes. — Large VOLUME of people.
ESCALATORS
Access to existing bldg.
VARIABLE SECONDARY STAIRS

PLATFORM

MAGNE

094c

4

ARCADE — Shelter, Protection
INFORMATION — advertising
SERIES of STRUCTURES
A SECOND 'STREET' Threshold.

ARCADE

094d

5

Series of MOVEABLE DECKS
WALKWAY + OBSERVATION
TEMPORARY HOLDING —
MOVING.

CAUSWAY

094e

094a, b, c, d, e. 1-5 magnets and notes
095. MAGNET - sketch

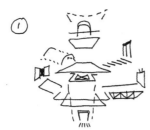

① Temporary protection
Length of index — STEPS, STAIRS,
— short-haul LIFT —

Size of   Resting AREA   **STAIRWAYS**
platforms —   Observation AREA

Ease of access   — Hanging around
Ease of change of level   Space - safely.

Threshold safety — NOT MUCH ground level
congregation

094a

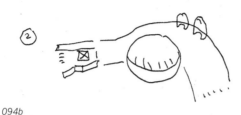

② Ease of access
VIEWING & ENJOYING   **PROMENADE**
Safety.
Ref. to small information

094b

③ Platform OBSERVATION — with SAFETY   **PLATFORM**
Cross-routes. — Large VOLUME of people.
ESCALATORS
ACCESS to existing bldg.   **MAGNE**
VARIABLE SECONDARY STAIRS

094c

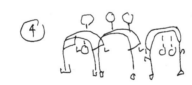

④ ARCADE — Shelter, Protection
INFORMATION — advertising   **ARCADE**
SERIES of STRUCTURES
A SECOND 'STREET' Threshold.

094d

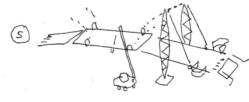

⑤ Series of MOVEABLE DECKS
WALKWAY + OBSERVATION **CAUSWAY**
TEMPORARY HOLDING —
MOVING.

094e

094a, b, c, d, e. 1-5 magnets and notes
095. MAGNET - sketch

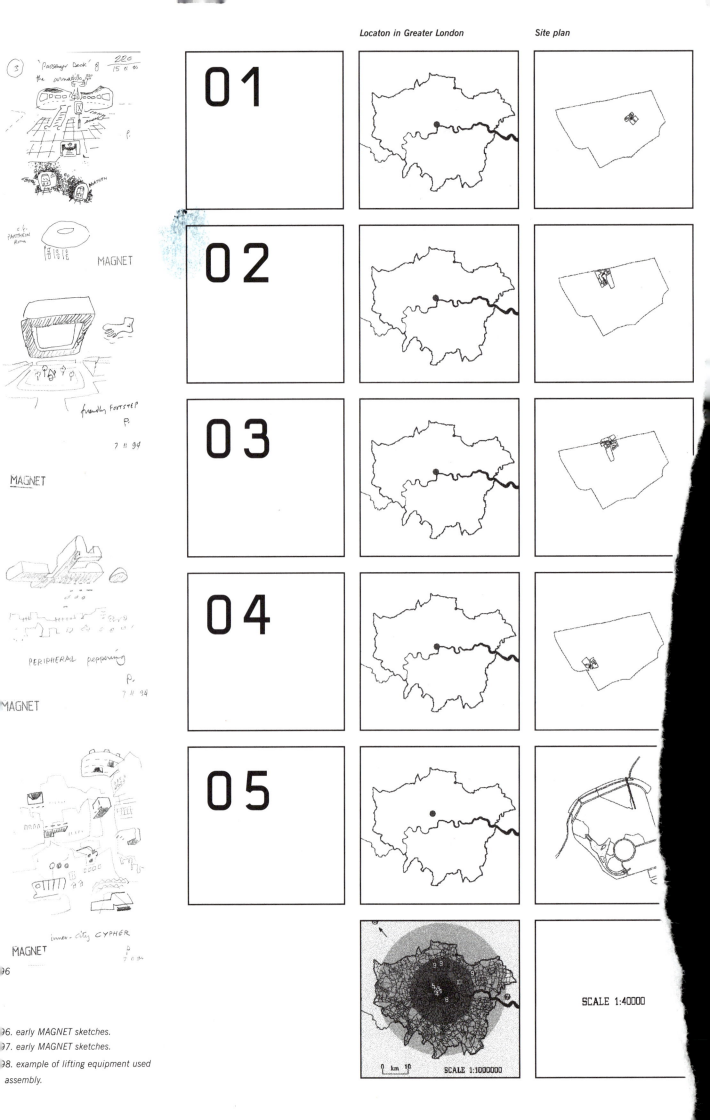

Locaton in Greater London

Site plan

01

02

03

04

05

SCALE 1:1000000

SCALE 1:40000

96. early MAGNET sketches.
97. early MAGNET sketches.
98. example of lifting equipment used
assembly.

MAGNET

MAGNET

MAGNET

MAGNET

inner-city CYPHER

MAGNET

PERIPHERAL peppering

friendly FOOTSTEP

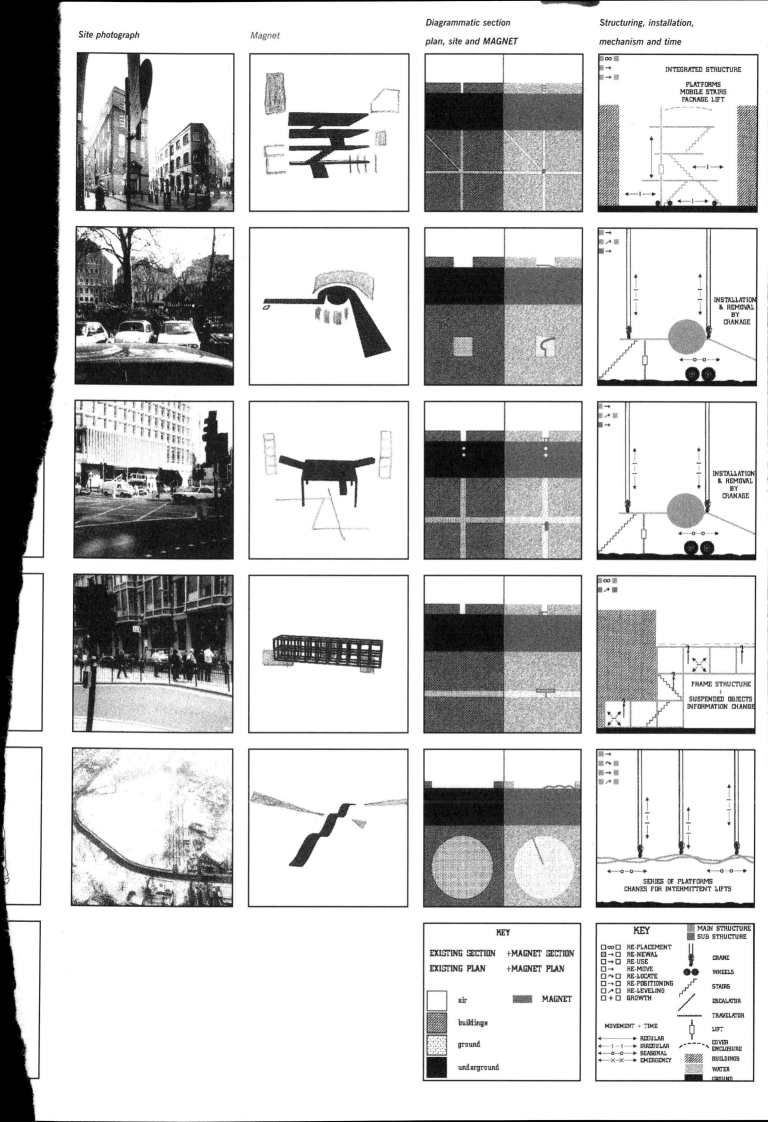

Site photograph *Magnet* *Diagrammatic section plan, site and MAGNET* *Structuring, installation, mechanism and time*

INTEGRATED STRUCTURE
PLATFORMS
MOBILE STAIRS
PACKAGE LIFT

INSTALLATION & REMOVAL BY CRANAGE

INSTALLATION & REMOVAL BY CRANAGE

FRAME STRUCTURE + SUSPENDED OBJECTS INFORMATION CHANGE

SERIES OF PLATFORMS
CRANES FOR INTERMITTENT LIFTS

KEY

EXISTING SECTION +MAGNET SECTION
EXISTING PLAN +MAGNET PLAN

air
buildings
ground
underground

MAGNET

KEY

□∞□ RE-PLACEMENT
⊠→□ RE-NEWAL
□→□ RE-USE
□→ RE-MOVE
□∧□ RE-LOCATE
□→□ RE-POSITIONING
□↗□ RE-LEVELING
□+□ GROWTH

MOVEMENT + TIME
→ REGULAR
—I—I— IRREGULAR
—o—o— SEASONAL
—x—x— EMERGENCY

MAIN STRUCTURE
SUB STRUCTURE
CRANE
WHEELS
STAIRS
ESCALATOR
TRAVELATOR
LIFT
COVER ENCLOSURE
BUILDINGS
WATER
GROUND

MAGNET

MAGNETS are installed on existing metropolitan sites which are at present UNDERUSED or MISUSED.

Their SITING enriches the intensity of the city grain.

The STRUCTURES act as both INSERTS AND TRANSPLANTS providing socially beneficial movement routes. Their PLANNING encourages adjacent future growth while the FIXED-LIFE structures enable VARIATION & RE-ASSEMBLY to be undertaken with speed and minimal disruption.

To establish a valid equation between contemporary social aspirations and Architecture, it is essential to add to the latter Doubt, Delight and Change as design criteria.

MAGNETS are an example of the necessity of Anticipatory Design.

Cedric price 15.3.'96

090

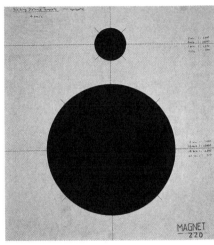

091

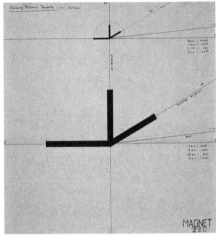

092

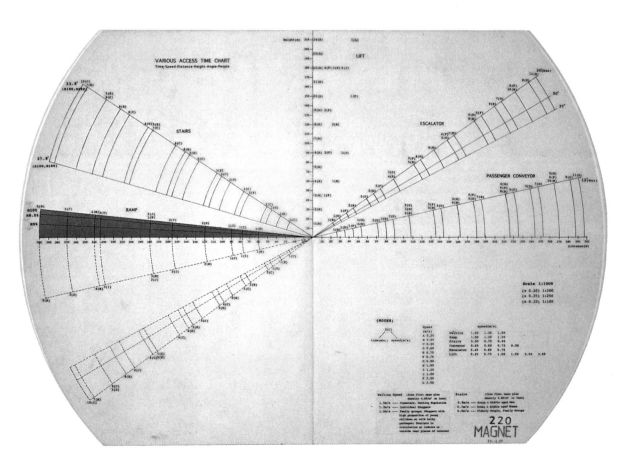

093

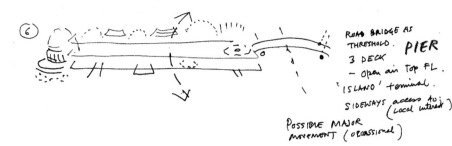

(6)

ROAD BRIDGE AS
THRESHOLD. **PIER**
3 DECK
— Open air Top FL.
'ISLAND' terminal.
SIDEWAYS access to;
(Local interest)

POSSIBLE MAJOR
MOVEMENT (occassional)

099a

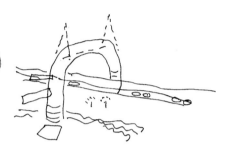

ARCH

STRESSES BRIDGE with TORSION
VERTICAL DOMINANCE
Water 'BASES' — OBSERVATION
ACCESS WALKWAYS — interim

MAGNET

099b

(8)

ROOF LEVEL
WALKWAY +
CONTEMPLATION
Corridor — access
& stability — helped
by EXISTING BLDGS.
CITY GRID CHANGE
A SECOND STREET — NEW
Possible CRANE Support
LONG TERM

TRANSPORTER

099c

A SECOND STREET — NEW
Possible CRANE Support
LONG TERM

(9)

Neigahood
BLANKET
BROADWAY
at 90° to original
Course for LAND)
USE) NEW

'CITY' SQUARE

099d

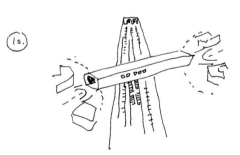

(10.)

A NEW VARIED
DEVEL GENERATOR
of the entire AREA
A NEW
CITY STARTER
varied directional
feeds. MAGNET

MAGNET

MAGNET

099e

M. 220   12.11.94

∴ 'Uneven' or cantilevered inserts (2)
(smart materials?
"Learning where to
settle down.")

[CP/AJ]

MAGNET →

Continuous
structural
integrity until 'fixed'

"IN BETWEEN HOOKS" ? cf. Sky scrapers / foundation

100

230
HALMAG

An application of 220 to an actual and difficult sloping site; Sheffield Hallam University. The project investigates ways of negotiating a safer route between town centre and the train station, via the University, "providing a variety of structural city links".

Former Chancellor of the University, Sir Norman Adsetts, is acknowledged for his support of this work.

"The Sheffield Links differ from the original Magnets in that they make new public facilities out of existing amenities rather than inventing new ones."

Kester Rattenbury, "The Power of Attraction", **BD***, 30 April 1999.*

This page:
105. site plan.
Opposite:
106. Sheffield magnet.
107. sketch site plan highlighting network and links.
108. sketch section through site indicating new means of access between buildings.

HALMAG	SCALE	DB 230	DRAWING X003
CONFIDENTIAL		SHEFFIELD HALLAM UNIVERSITY MAGNET	

0114 253 2092 Fx 20502 T SUZANNE CASS

TO FURTHER EXTEND THE UNIVERSITY'S LEARNING CAPABILITY TO THE CITY & BEYOND
CREATING A NEW 'UNIVERSITY SITE' FOR EXCHANGE AND INFORMATION WHILE EN RICHING THE PUBLICS EASE OF MOBILITY, SAFETY & DELIGHT. +
PROVIDING A PUBLIC/ UNIVERSITY FOOTBRIDGE AVAILABLE 24-WS FOR ALL LINKING THE MAJOR CENTRE CITY WORK, RECREATION & MOVEMENT ZONES.

A high-level, all weather bridge spanning from the University to Supertram, and providing pedestrian access to both sides of Sheaf St. & points throughout the Station
A network of information feeds is integrated into the structure.

SUCH A LINK CAN GENERATE FURTHER DESIRED CITY & UNIVERSITY LINKS & ACT AS A MAGNET FOR FURTHER DEVELOPMENT
[+ disabled access thr'out]

CEDRIC PRICE MA Cantab. ARIBA AA Dipl. ARCHITECT
38 ALFRED PLACE LONDON WC1E 7DP Tel: 01-636-5220

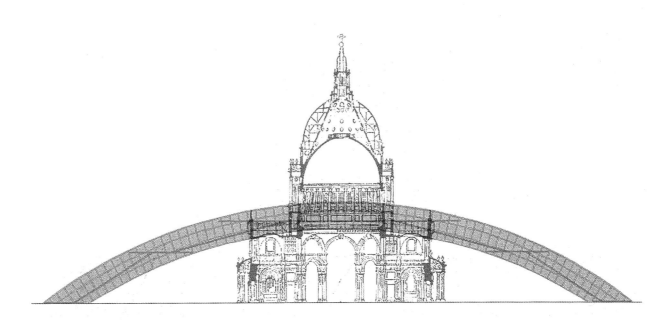

Assumption ?

K- Ass
Keilah's Assumption

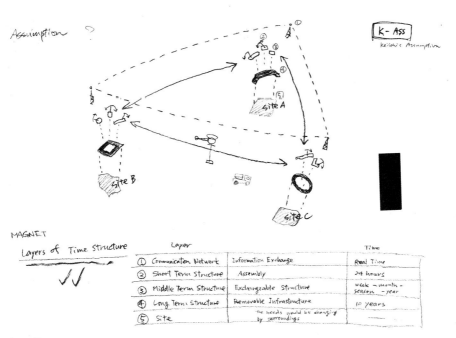

site A

site B

site C

MAGNET

Layers of Time Structure
√√

	Layer		Time
① Communication Network	Information Exchange		Real Time
② Short Term Structure	Assembly		24 hours
③ Middle Term Structure	Exchangeable Structure		week – month – season – year
④ Long Term Structure	Removable Infrastructure		10 years
⑤ Site	the needs would be changing by surroundings		———

5. Sep. 95   K.S

06			
07			
08			
09			
10			

SCALE 1:1000000

SCALE 1:40000

Magnet

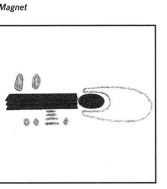

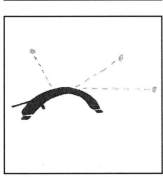

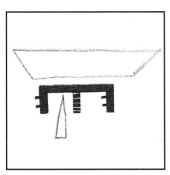

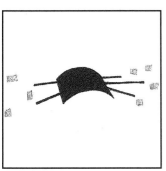

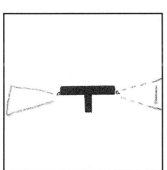

Diagrammatic section
plan, site and MAGNET

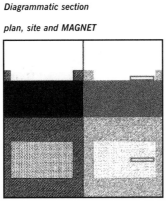

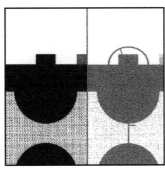

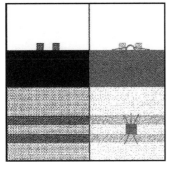

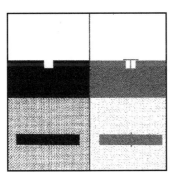

Structuring, installation,
mechanism and time

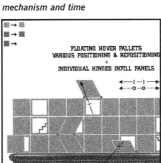

FLOATING HOVER PALLETS
VARIOUS POSITIONING & REPOSITIONING
+
INDIVIDUAL HINGED INFILL PANELS

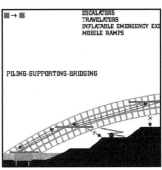

ESCALATORS
TRAVELATORS
INFLATABLE EMERGENCY EXIT
MOBILE RAMPS

PILING-SUPPORTING-BRIDGING

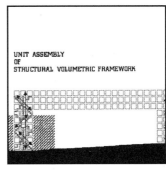

UNIT ASSEMBLY
OF
STRUCTURAL VOLUMETRIC FRAMEWORK

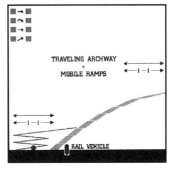

TRAVELING ARCHWAY
+
MOBILE RAMPS

RAIL VEHICLE

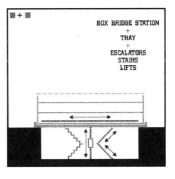

BOX BRIDGE STATION
+
TRAY
+
ESCALATORS
STAIRS
LIFTS

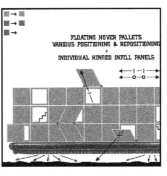

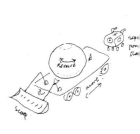

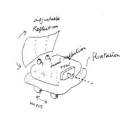

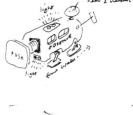

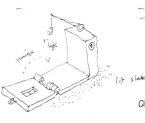

KEY

EXISTING SECTION   +MAGNET SECTION

EXISTING PLAN   +MAGNET PLAN

- air
- buildings
- ground
- underground

MAGNET

KEY

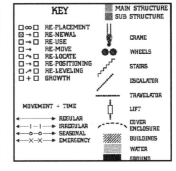

- □∞□ RE-PLACEMENT
- ⊠→□ RE-NEWAL
- □→□ RE-USE
- □→□ RE-MOVE
- □∧□ RE-LOCATE
- □⊙□ RE-POSITIONING
- □↗□ RE-LEVELING
- □+□ GROWTH

MOVEMENT + TIME

- ←——→ REGULAR
- ←-I-I→ IRREGULAR
- ←-o-o→ SEASONAL
- ←-X-X→ EMERGENCY

MAIN STRUCTURE
SUB STRUCTURE

- CRANE
- WHEELS
- STAIRS
- ESCALATOR
- TRAVELATOR
- LIFT
- COVER ENCLOSURE
- BUILDINGS
- WATER
- GROUND

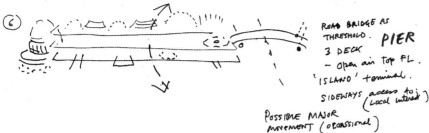

⑥

ROAD BRIDGE AS
THRESHOLD. **PIER**
3 DECK
– Open air Top FL.
'ISLAND' terminal.
SIDEWAYS access to;
(Local interest)

POSSIBLE MAJOR
MOVEMENT (occassional)

099a

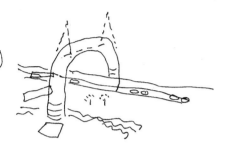

ARCH

STRESSES BRIDGE with TORSION.
VERTICAL DOMINANCE
Water 'BASES' – OBSERVATION
ACCESS WALKWAYS – interim

MAGNET

099b

⑧

ROOF LEVEL
WALKWAY +
CONTEMPLATION
Corridor – access
E stability – helped
by EXISTING BLDGS.

TRANSPORTER

CITY GROWN GRID CHANGE
A SECOND STREET – NEW
Possible CRANE Support
LONG TERM

099c

A SECOND STREET – NEW
Possible CRANE Support
LONG TERM

⑨

Neighborhood
BLANKET
BROADWAY
at 90° to original
Course for LAND
USE ; NEW

'CITY' SQUARE

099d

⑩

A NEW VARIED
DEVEL GENERATOR
of the entire AREA
A NEW
CITY STARTER
varied directional
feeds. MAGNET

MAGNET

MAGNET

099e

m. 220   12.11.94

'Uneven' or cantilevered inserts ②
(smart materials?
"Learning where to
settle down.")

[CP/AS
article]

MAGNET →

continuous
structural
integrity until 'fixed'

"IN BETWEEN HOOKS" ? cf.> Sky Scrapers / foundation   100

X27
WALSALL

A competition for a new city centre bus station.

The bus has its own roof – CPA is concerned with the business of looking after the passengers getting on and off the bus (ref. 190) requiring a study of the flow; when the molecules (buses) are static and the particles (people) keep moving.

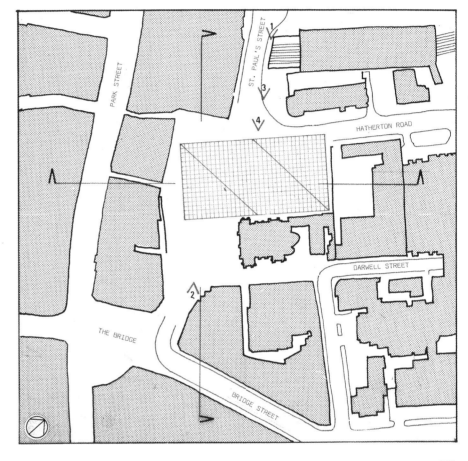

103

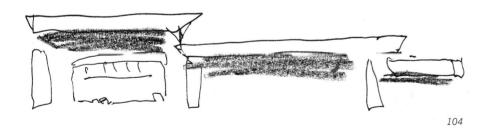

104

"The ability to 'see' time is as important as that of 'hearing' space (in Dr Richard Gregory's terms). The radial-fingered clock enables one to visualize twenty minutes as a slice of time that is large enough for a useful conversation or a quiet drink." Computers, AA Files, no.19.

103. roof plan showing position and orientation on site.
104. sketch elevation showing tiered roof levels.

230
HALMAG

An application of 220 to an actual
and difficult sloping site; Sheffield Hallam
University. The project investigates
ways of negotiating a safer route between
town centre and the train station,
via the University, "providing a variety
of structural city links".

Former Chancellor of the University,
Sir Norman Adsetts, is acknowledged for
his support of this work.

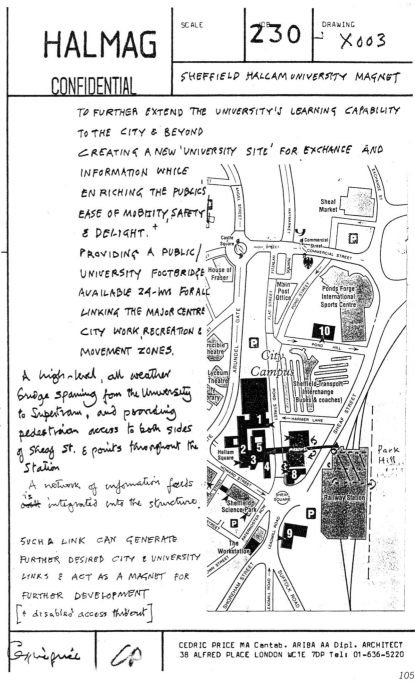

HALMAG

CONFIDENTIAL

SCALE

JOB **230**

DRAWING X003

SHEFFIELD HALLAM UNIVERSITY MAGNET

0114 253 2042 Fx SUZANNE CASS
T 0505

TO FURTHER EXTEND THE UNIVERSITY'S LEARNING CAPABILITY
TO THE CITY & BEYOND
CREATING A NEW 'UNIVERSITY SITE' FOR EXCHANGE AND
INFORMATION WHILE
ENRICHING THE PUBLICS
EASE OF MOBILITY, SAFETY
& DELIGHT. +
PROVIDING A PUBLIC/
UNIVERSITY FOOTBRIDGE
AVAILABLE 24-HRS FORALL
LINKING THE MAJOR CENTRE
CITY WORK, RECREATION &
MOVEMENT ZONES.

A high-level, all weather
bridge spanning from the University
to Supertram, and providing
pedestrian access to both sides
of Sheaf St. & points throughout the
Station

A network of information feeds
is
outh integrated into the structure.

SUCH A LINK CAN GENERATE
FURTHER DESIRED CITY & UNIVERSITY
LINKS & ACT AS A MAGNET FOR
FURTHER DEVELOPMENT
[+ disabled access throout]

CEDRIC PRICE MA Cantab. ARIBA AA Dipl. ARCHITECT
38 ALFRED PLACE LONDON WC1E 7DP Tel: 01-636-5220

105

"The Sheffield Links differ from the original
Magnets in that they make new public facilities
out of existing amenities rather than inventing
new ones."

Kester Rattenbury, "The Power of Attraction",
***BD**, 30 April 1999.*

This page:
105. site plan.
Opposite:
106. Sheffield magnet.
107. sketch site plan highlighting network and links.
108. sketch section through site indicating
new means of access between buildings.

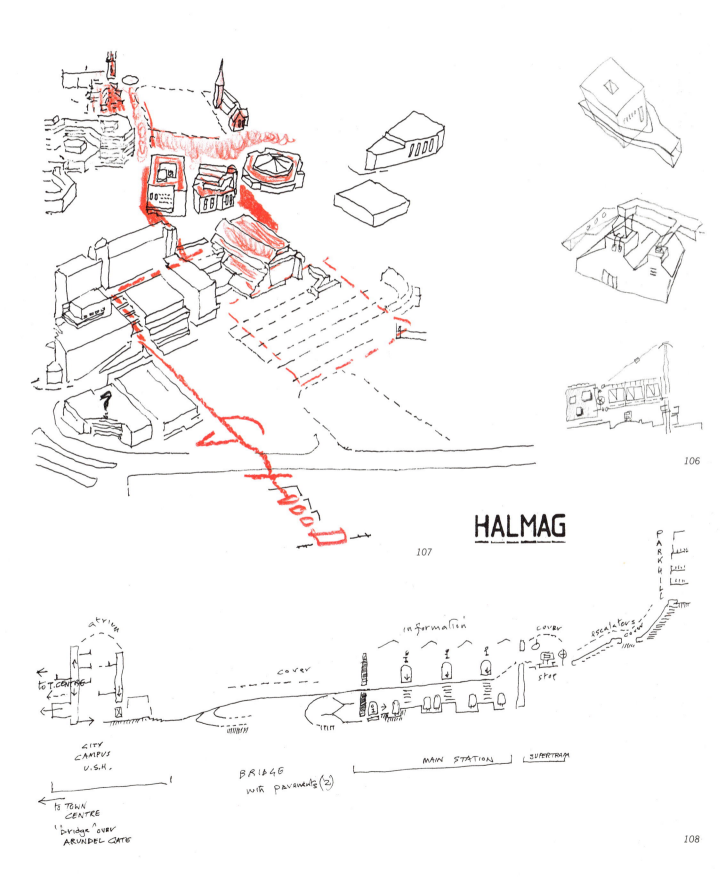

HALMAG

107

106

atrium

information

cover

P A R K H I L L

cover

escalators down

stop

to T.CENTRE

CITY
CAMPVS
U.S.H.

BRIDGE
with pavements (2)

MAIN STATION | SUPERTRAM

to TOWN
CENTRE

"bridge" over
ARUNDEL GATE

108

7 — THERE AND GONE

M | 245 VENICE | 221 TATE MODERN | 180 WESTAL | 244 IFPRI | 241 MEAN | 239 CROWBAR

"SPACE AS SPEED IN TIME"

TRIED AND TESTED
USED AND FINISHED

SIZE AND DISTANCE
REPETITION
RE-THINK
RE-USE
PRESERVE
RE-NEW
RE-USE (AGAIN AND AGAIN)
REPLACE
RE-THINK

REJECT

REFLECT AND RECONSIDER
REJECT - AGAIN

REPLACE

REPLAN

SOCIAL
SOCIETY - NEW

"YOU NEED TIME"

7–

THERE
AND
GONE

239
CROWBAR

The first and only commission by Crowbar Coffee Ltd. for drawings on paper cups. Print run: 10,000 and sold (only containing coffee) at three coffee bars in East and Central London.

This world message on a cup reads:

"If then we represent our Earth as a little ball of one inch diameter then the Sun would be a big globe nine foot across and 323 yards away, that is about a fifth of a mile, four or five minutes walking."

Cedric Price aka H.G.Wells.

109

109. Crowbar paper cup with printed message.

180
WESTAL

Prototypes for three mobile market stalls developed for Westminster City Council (WCC). To be tested in Berwick Street and Tachbrook Street Markets. The prototypes: a trolley for fruit and vegetables, a stall for hanging clothes and fabric, and a kiosk for magazines and nick-nacks, were built by Slingsby for inclusion in their catalogue. At the time of publication, there are three stalls (still in perfect condition) available for sale.

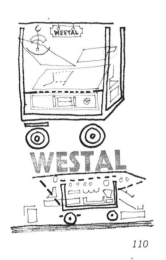

110

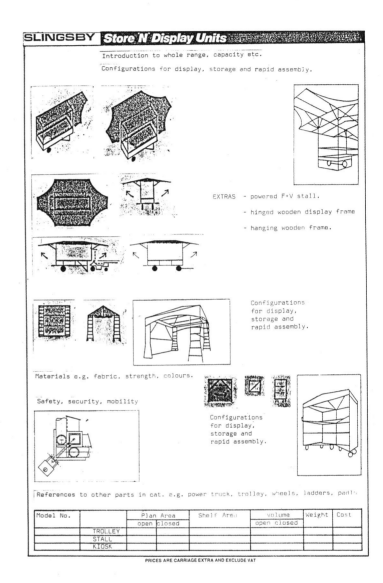

111

112

110. sketch of fruit and vegetable stall.
111. mock-up page for the Slingsby Catalogue.
112. photograph, detail of prototype stall.

241
MEAN

An exhibition, "Cedric Price: Mean Time" at the Canadian Centre for Architecture (CCA), Montreal.

Price devised fourteen icons for "fourteen ways to look at time" to accompany his selection of fifty-four objects drawn from the collection of the CCA. Fourteen examples are shown on these pages.

The catalogue reads: "Price draws upon the collection of the CCA to develop… complex relationships between time, movement, and space and invite(s) us to observe how it acts in the built environment. At the same time, he uses these objects and images to draw attention to our failure to consider the relationship adequately. Mean Time presents… constructions in which time is measured through space, where movement is controlled and synchronized by structure, where spatial constraints are overcome by simultaneity, where time is distorted and distance deceptive, where the structure depicts its own demise, or where efforts to anticipate social conditions have proved either strangely prescient or woefully wrong."

Self-Destruction
54 "Millennium 'river of fire' will be visible from space"
The Independent (London) 27 July 1999
Life expectancy of event described: 10.8 seconds
Life expectancy of this document when exposed for exhibition: opinions vary, but short
Revisit the exhibition in two months to find out how mean time is

Refabrication
34 Cedric Price
Great Britain; born Stone, Staffordshire, 1934
Plan, elevations, perspectives, and details for a demountable and transportable archaeologist's house: student project, University of Cambridge School of Architecture 1952-53
Pen and black ink on woven paper
55.6 x 76.5 cm

Prediction
45 Marshall McLuhan
Canada; Edmonton1911-Toronto 1980
Distant Early Warning playing cards, from a game invented by McLuhan to test powers of anticipation
Copyright 1969
Offset lithograph
Cards 8.8 x 5.7 cm, box 9.5 x 6.4 cm

Anticipating the Impossible
24 Wenzel Hablik
Brux, Bohemia, 1881 – Itzehoe, Germany, 1934
Drawing for a domed structure sent to members of the "Crystal Chain" between 1919 and 1920
Mimeographic copy on woven paper
21 x 33 cm

Chronicle
2 Natale Bonifacio, engraver
Croatia; Sibernik, Dalmatia 1538-1592
Giovanni Guerra, draftsman Italy; Modena 1540 – Rome 1618
The lowering and transportation of the Vatican obelisk, 1586
Engraving on laid paper
52 x 115.1 cm
Published in March 1586, prerecording on a single sheet an event that actually took place over a month later and continued for nearly four months.

Synchronization

10 Gustave Le Gray
Villiers-le-Bel, France, 1820 – Cairo, Egypt, 1882
Railroad yard, Tours, France 1851
Albumen silver print from waxed – paper negative
25.3 x 34.9 cm (image); 32.7 x 42.6 cm (sheet)
Several sets of railroad cars are laid on tracks that run through train sheds
and converge at a rotating platform used to turn engines and lead them to a
single route.

Interval

21 C.W. Scott
Active c.1906
The Dioptric Apparatus
Relief halftone
30.7 x 25 cm
Plate following page 30 in **History of the Fastnet Rock Lighthouses**
(London: Hazell, Watson & Viney, 1906).

Simultaneous

28 Unknown photographer
The Shabolovsky Broadcasting Station aerial tower
Moscow 1931
Relief halftone, postcard stock
9.4 x 13.8 cm (image, irreg.); 10.7 x 14.8 cm (sheet, irreg.)

Uncertainty

52 Jan Groover
Born Plainfield, New Jersey, 1943
West Side Highway, New York City (built 1937-48, closed 1973,
reused as a recreation and art space 1973-81, demolished 1981)
October 1981
Platinum/palladium print
26.2 x 33.9 cm (image); 28.2 x 37 cm (sheet)

The Pleasure of Frustration

44 Cedric Price
Great Britain; born Stone, Staffordshire, 1934
Plan and elevation of a maze for Port Eliot, Cornwall, England 1966
Black ink on mylar
59 x 71.9 cm
Accompanied by an aerial photograph, c.1990.
Courtesy of Earl St. Germans

Suspending Time

20 Arnold Genthe
Berlin, Germany, 1869 – New Milford, Connecticut, 1942
General view of the aftermath of the 1906 earthquake and fire, looking down
Market Street from the Ferry Building Tower, San Francisco, California 1906
Gelatin silver print
18.9 x 24.2 cm

Distorting Time

37 Office ofSkidmore, Owings & Merrill, Chicago
Architects and Engineers
Myron Goldsmith, Senior Designer
Sections for the Robert R. McMath Solar Telescope,
Kitt Peak National Observatory, Kitt Peak, Arizona 3 June 1959
Graphite and blue pencil on vellum
76.5 x 102 cm
"At the top of the concrete tower, a 2-meter (82 inch) flat mirror directs the
sunlight downward to an angle of 32 degrees. At the bottom of the 500 foot
shaft, a 1.5 meter (60 inch) image-forming mirror reflects the beam back up the
shaft. At ground level, a third mirror catches the beam and sends it into the
observing room, where the image of the sun is formed on a horizontal table."

Gravity

39 Konrad Wachsmann
Germany and United States; Frankfurt an der Oder 1901
Los Angeles, California, 1980
Side view of the tetrahedral space structure of a bicycle frame.
Relief halftone
26.2 x 23.1 cm
Page 47 in **The Turning Point of Building** *(New York: Reinhold Publishing*
Corporation, 1961)

Pacing

53 J.Rush Inc, Agincourt, Ontario
3500 Series Revolving Doors
Colour halftone offset lithograph
28 x 42.9 cm (page)
Pages 15-16 in C.J. Rush Inc. **Entrances** *(Agincourt, Ontario,c.1985)*

244
IFPRI

The first international ideas
competition run by the Canadian Centre
for Architecture (CCA).
Site: West Side, Manhattan.

Cities have a future dependent on their growth and change,
together with the quality of their occupancy. New York City
has a particular nature, which is "Pride in the New".
The unique bears no comparison.

New York City is ideally suited to the opportunity of
establishing a new quality of the 21st century which must be
shared by all its citizens and enjoyed by its visitors.
Such a quality should be recognized to be beneficial to all.
New York City is strong and generous enough to achieve this.
The quality is — comprehensive and continuous improvement of
its citizens' health.

Mental, physical and sensory well-being are required.
Such a quality may well constitute the future definition of
the 21st century city.

The site chosen for the first IFCCA competition is ideal for
such a crucial working, living test.

The timing is critical — opportunity is unique and will occur
once only. A strategy for cities will be established.

A lung for Mid-town is provided.

The Hudson River is the primary intake. The 'open-air' quality
of the site must be realised. The present FALLOW element
of the SITE should be exploited. Railway lines should remain
uncovered and a geotechnic survey be undertaken to determine
surface drainage patterns and future land movements. Redundant
high-level tracks should be demolished with immediacy.
Both weeds and planners (sic)"inedible greenery" should be
excluded. The hard nature of Manhattan's man-made surfaces
should be recognized and maintained. Fortuitously, the
nature of the current land-owners is beneficial to the
successful execution of this proposal. The future may suggest
new forms of co-operation between differing bodies — public
and private, city, state and national — united by their
common desire for land.

Pressure for housing accommodation both from the adjacent
community and from the ever-hungry NEW YORK UNIVERSITY should
not be ignored.

FUTURE DELIGHT OF THE SITE - The views of distance, the
ability to walk across the site, the awareness of seasonal
change, the awareness of a 24 hour cycle, the clean smell,
the cleanliness of the Hudson, aspirations of fish farming
there, the valid social life-span of all new structures
realised in design...

Skidmore, Owings & Merrill's Lever House
building in New York City was described on
completion in 1952 as 'a city lung'.

Opposite:
113. competition entry drawing.
114. letter to CP from film director, Mike Nichols.

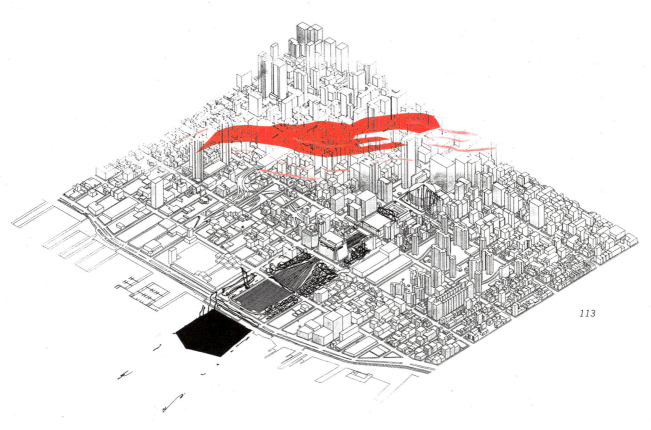

113

MIKE NICHOLS

October 19, 1999

Dear Cedric,

I spent a very happy hour last week in contemplation of your design for the West Side Redevelopment. I was quite moved by its wit and simplicity, by the vision of the sweetness it could bring to all of Manhattan. I looked again and again at the beauty of the railway tracks and walked again and again back and forth between your wit and the ponderousness and pretension of the Skidmore's and the rest of them.

Then, yesterday, there was the Muschamp article in The Times. I think it's only the beginning. I think that a clear and beautiful idea becomes politically stronger and stronger with time. I think you have done something really important.

I noted, as well, your kind and undeserved thanks to me. It is my turn now. I thank you for something that a lot of us Manhattan dwellers will be unable to forget.

All the best,

Mike

221
TATE MODERN

An international design
competition, London.

STATEMENT ON THE ROLE OF CULTURAL CENTRES IN THE 21ST CENTURY

The real wealth of any nation is best judged by the knowledge
and well-being of its individual citizens. The resultant
dreams, delights and interest are the basis of culture at any
single time. Both the aspirations to explore, make and
achieve, and those to identify, understand and consume require
time to progress. Culture has an essential constituent of
change-through-time.

It is in the making and consuming that culture is created,
not in the identifying, classifying and storage.

A centre for culture may allow for these disparate conditions
to thrive and flourish through both protection and exposure.

Cultural growth may be achieved on a finite site while its
fruitful dissemination through retrieval is geographically
uncharitable. However, "making the best available to the most"
remains an admirable, if rough, definition of such a place.

Today the exercising and enjoyment of cultural mores of
whatever form, tend to generate in age groups rather than
this demarked by nationality or wealth.

Such grouping in appetite for, production and appreciation of
various cultural mores will, inevitably, be succeeded by
further demarkation.

This continuous rhythm of changing cultures should be enabled,
rather than merely be mirrored by a 'cultural centre'.

A valid cultural centre must create conditions of communal and
private delight, productivity and appreciation previously
unimaginable.

The three-dimensional contribution to these aims is a measure
of Architecture's usefulness. An exploitive use by such a
centre, of the seasons, the weather and the 24 hour clock is
more important than the realisation of pure form through
visual activity.

The periphery of such a centre is four dimensional in which
Time is the key dimension in access and retrieval related to
people, energy and data. This periphery depends on the social
and economic usefulness it provides. In the 21st century, this
is unlikely to be charitable. It will be recognised rather by
life-enhancing services it provides.

A 21st century 'cultural centre' will utilize calculated
uncertainty and unconscious incompleteness to produce a
catalyst for invigorating change whilst always producing the
"harvest of the silent eye". Cedric Price 14 March 1994.

115. competition entry drawing.

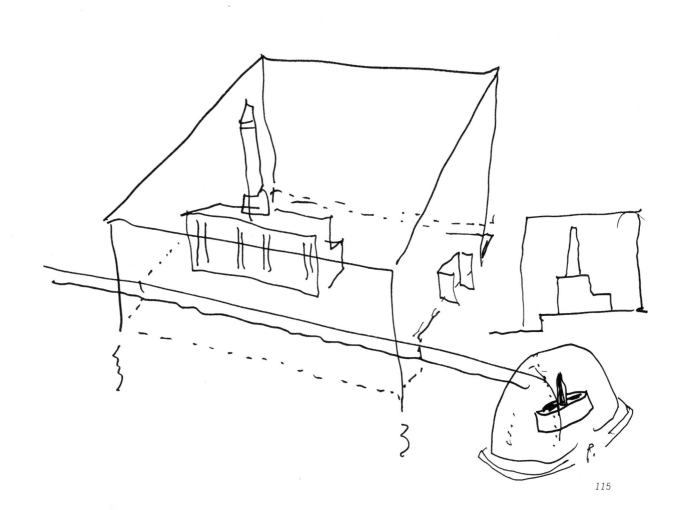

115

245
VENICE' 01

Having initially accepted the invitation to participate in the Venice Biennale, on reading the list of other participants, CPA subsequently declined. At that time Price made this presentation for his "own delight".

The exhibit MUST occur in REAL TIME in relation to this INTENT. Therefore this exhibit ITSELF must question all who visit - in the experience of the enjoyment of a 'virtual' future 'CITY'. The very word CITY is insufficient to describe the MULTIFARIOUS EXPERIENCES (social & sensorial) that occur NOW and in the FUTURE. Therefore C.P. proposes to replace CITY with CONCENTRATE being the concentration of people in one place for an UNSPECIFIED TIME.

TIME is the FOURTH DIMENSION of ARCHITECTURE - and must always be included in a VALID ARCHITECTURE CODE. "ARCHITECTURE IS THAT WHICH, THROUGH THE DISTORTION OF TIME, CREATES SOCIALLY BENEFICIAL CONDITIONS HITHERTO IMPOSSIBLE."

C.Price 1964.

LESSONS FOR THE FUTURE:

the role of the city, suburbs and periphery as 'test beds'. A Futures' Directory becomes continuously available to ALL. The operation of this project should, through its operational delight, give both a taste and an appetite to all those who STAND & STARE. With increasing world-wide passive surveillance techniques (satellites, photography, thermal, geographic, scanning etc.) a directory could become available - in TIME - to act. GLOBAL CONSTRUCTIVE CITIZENRY becomes universal FUN. To humanize KNOWLEDGE and make it more APPETIZING.

...they say you cannot design infinity, but if you look at railway lines and think that somewhere they meet, then that is a definition of infinity.

116

This page:
116. sketch of scene in Venice by CP c.1950s.
Opposite:
117. the city as an egg.
118. proposal imagined Venice for Biennale.
119. aerial view of Angkor Wat (above) compared with that of Venice (beneath).

ref: "The City Form and Intent" being a collection of 50 significant towns and cities all to the same scale, 1:14,400, By Richard Saul Wurman and 61 students from the School of Design, student publication volume 13. No.'s 1 and 2, University of South Caroliner, Raleigh, 1963.

Opposite:
120. ref: J.J. Grandville, "The Flâneur of the Universe". A satrical illustration of the popular vision of the St. Simeon view of progress through the development of universal communications. Here the planets are united by an iron bridge, lit by observation galleries of iron and glass ring the earth, allowing uninterrupted vision of the solar system. From "On Streets", ed. Stanford Anderson (MIT).
121. ref: Harmsworth Monthly Pictorial Magazine, Volume 3, Augaust 1889 – January 1900, Harmsworth Bros. Ltd. London EC.

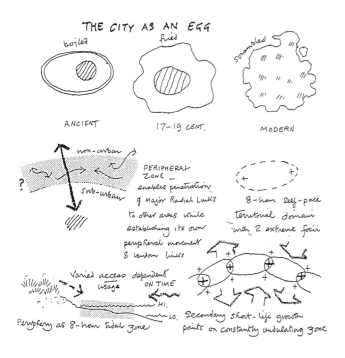

THE CITY AS AN EGG

boiled — ANCIENT

fried — 17-19 CENT.

scrambled — MODERN

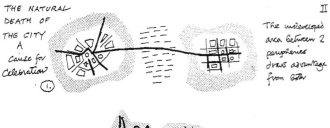

non-urban
?
sub-urban

PERIPHERAL ZONE — enables penetration of Major Radial Links to other areas while establishing its own peripheral movement & random links

8-hour self-pace territorial domain with 2 extreme focii

Varied access dependent ON TIME usage

HI.

LO.

Periphery as 8-hour tidal zone

Secondary short-life growth points on constantly undulating zone

THE NATURAL DEATH OF THE CITY A Cause for Celebration

II

The undeveloped area between 2 peripheries draws advantage from both

NOTE! The densely populated internally congested island state

... the national periphery with 50% below water,

117

(Note: An unglazed opening providing a clear view of VENICE enable visual comparisons with see through imagery)

118

119

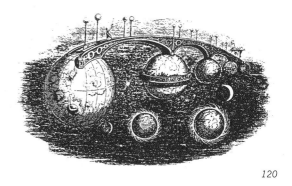

120

IF LONDON WERE LIKE VENICE

121

M̄

A message, translated into two forms
of Chinese and distributed at the 'M'
conference in Beijing. A live amplified
telephone link between Price in his offices
in London and Irata Isozaki, present at
the conference, relayed questions from
the audience.

<u>ON 'M'</u>

Propulsion is the progression in time enabling anticipation
of a process whose very speed is measurable and which,
when anticipated, can become a useful scale of social
anticipation.   This can then be compared to other forms
of measurement, e.g. the speed of motorized flight, or the
movement of the finger on a clock's face.

This unification of relative speeds enables the 'speed' of a
building to be considered jointly with an anticipated period
of peace.

The anticipated water levels of the Three Gorges Dam
can then be allotted particular speeds.

The speeds of a particular anticipated flight south from
Beijing can be compared with the social benefits of mobile
telephones on the same scale; as could the exclusion of
motorised noise to the health of the young of future cities.

The relationship between power end energy will still pose
a question of storage, whether behind a dam or in a dry
battery or a gymnasium.   But at least the time factor is of
the same nature.

→ M - Movement is still critical

    as are: Motive
                 Motivation
                 Mystery
                 Magic

COPY

The last is the greatest.

This page:
*122. copy of 'the 'M'essage' with note on string
theory related to a question from the audience.*
Opposite:
Cedric Price in Milton Keynes, 1995.

c.f " String theory "

Cedric Price
BEJING
MAYDAY 2002

122

PAUL FINCH

—

*Paul Finch Hon FRIBA entered journalism in 1972. He was deputy editor of **Estates Times**, (1976-1983), editor of **Building Design**, (1983-1994) and editor of the **Architects' Journal** (1994-99). He is currently editorial director of the publishing group EMAP Construct and contributes to a wide range of forums as a commentator on architecture and design. He is Deputy Chairman of the Commission for Architecture and the Built Environment (CABE) and received an OBE in 2002.*

Cedric Price: the person in whose company time is passed quickest.

I started visiting Cedric Price's Alfred Place office regularly in 1983, after taking over the editorial reins at *Building Design*. I had met Cedric before when Peter Murray was editor, and he contributed a regular column to the paper at that time[1]; over the next 11 years he continued to write for the magazine at different times in a series of different formats, but always in the same spot next to the editorial. When I moved to the *Architects' Journal*, Cedric did a year's worth of visual columns[2] that were fraught with potential production difficulties but came out rather well. The various columns were the occasion rather than the cause of our near-weekly meetings, which often involved cheese and tomato rolls from Sidoli, the cafe downstairs, and coffee and brandy from our host. On one memorable occasion, with the writer Jeremy Melvin, we consumed an elaborate Edwardian-style breakfast of vast proportion, with Cedric cooking bacon, eggs and lamb chops on a tiny hot-plate stove, washed down with, sequentially, bottles of champagne, Rioja and brandy. It began at 8am and concluded at 11.30 when I reeled round to give a lecture to unsuspecting AA summer school students, with Price and Melvin in tow as minders.

Alastair McAlpine memorably described his own breakfast meetings with Cedric as a form of mental gymnastics, "to get my mind in shape"[3]; in my case it was a review of events and people, architectural politics analysed, larded with terrific and usually unpublishable gossip about the great and the good, and Cedric's often hilarious and sporadically successful attempts to recall the names of who had said or done what in the not-so-recent past. One of the great things about the meetings was that they were funny. You generally left feeling more optimistic than when you arrived. Favourite repeated topics included castles; who precisely

worked for whom and when; the various histories of the 'This Is Tomorrow'[4] gang; what was going on at the AA and (sometimes) the RIBA; transport policy, particularly rail; demolition; water; the neglect of time as a consideration in most architectural and planning propositions; and reports from Cedric's pals around the world, keeping him very much in touch with whatever was hot or not.

Cedric's range of contacts and interests are compartmentalised. Who but he, since he is its founder and life president, knows the entire composition of his mysterious 'Hot Stuff Club'? A core team comprising Cedric, architect David Allford, engineer Frank Newby, Architectural Association chairman Alvin Boyarsky and brother David, until the untimely deaths of three of the group's members, would go on mystery trips annually, organised by a different member each year.

There was also a regular gang who would be summoned to celebrate the office birthday, Cedric's birthday, and Christmas. The format was a regular one for many years: it was held in the White Room (also known as East Grinstead, so that the office administrator could deter unwanted telephone callers with the intelligence that 'Mr Price is in East Grinstead today'). Guests would be given a lethal champagne cocktail (if they weren't careful), though various wines would be available. English Cheddar and ham (or Bath chaps) would be in good supply. In recent years the cast list would be Joan Littlewood and her assistant Peter Rankin, Roy Landau, David Price, John Randall, Paul Hyett, Teresa Pritchard, sometimes Jeremy Melvin, and sometimes Eleanor Bron, though she was just as likely to leave once the guests had arrived, quite possibly because she had heard it all before. These were stories about the office and its past, the funniest of which has always to be told by Cedric

and involves a Hungarian with a taste for explosives which had near fatal results for the office on at least one occasion. Paul Hyett, despite his eminence as RIBA president, would revert to his former role as office junior, sometimes being dispatched for more provisions. My part in proceedings would be to attempt to tell a joke that would make Joan Littlewood laugh. There would generally be a fixed time limit on proceedings – Cedric will always be a stickler for office procedure.

Cedric's dislike of communications from people he doesn't know by anything other than postage has resulted in the past in some rather non-standard office procedures. For example, at the Alfred Place office he had a fax machine for very special occasions, but it was located in the locked first-floor room which resembled a combination of office equipment repository and architect's office that had been trapped in a time capsule. (I was once asked to return a surveyor's tripod to the AA that he had borrowed 30 years before.) Nobody was supposed to know the fax number. Occasionally it would spit out messages, but Cedric would only see them if he had occasion to go into the room, which was not guaranteed on any specific day. Answer-phones and mobile phones are out of the question. For someone who anticipated, in GENERATOR and INTERACTION, much of the computer design developments of the following 25 years, it might seem odd that in Priceworld, the idea that an architect would work with a computer was almost improper.

Cedric likes mechanical or hand-operated gadgets. These have included a desk fan that had a water element that had to be kept in the office fridge overnight to provide the cooling device for when the fan was operated. His extensive rubber stamp collection. The main office fridge, a hymn to botulism, had a lock on it for no discernible reason, and was used largely as a shelf. The office library, an Aladdin's cave of material, employed a notation system known only to Cedric. He had one section called NF (Not Fileable) that prompted an Indian assistant to leave the office after his first day because he saw the initials and thought Cedric was a member of the National Front. For a socialist whose long connections with the Labour Party were regularly massaged with lunches at the Gay Hussar in Soho, haunt of Michael Foot and many of the brothers, this incident was the sort of minor farce that peppered his anecdotes.

The City Corporation, Cedric's office landlord, finally gave notice for him to vacate Alfred Place when the lease ended. The last Christmas drinks were in 2001. Cedric had not been very well, and Joan Littlewood ticked him off thoroughly for having the party. The trauma of leaving the office after forty two years has provided Cedric with the chance to behave somewhat like the Architecture Club[5], which he always admired for its refusal to inhabit any office at all. The club is where it meets. Cedric Price Architects is now wherever Cedric Price happens to be; the Royal Institute of British Architects at breakfast, St.John[6] for lunch, in a train travelling across Canada. Today, office procedure relies solely upon the postal service and a scheduled meeting – mobile phones and uninvited visitors still cause irritation.

The enjoyment of gossip, political analysis and thoughts on architecture continue to be the leitmotif of our meetings. For those who have had the chance to talk to Cedric directly about anything and everything, the main effect must be on the way one is moved to think afresh about issues, often realising that a Cedric way of looking at the world has rubbed off. It is not that the conclusions reached are necessarily the same as his, but the questions one asks oneself, and the way a problem (or a solution) is framed might well have something in common. The insights into time and anticipation, or the difference between tolerance and calculated inaccuracy, the aphorisms both original and quoted (his own 'necessary repetition for the wilfully inattentive'; and Sir Geoffrey Vicker's 'to be late is to be systematically wrong' – MAGNET) have stuck in my mind. While we occasionally travelled further afield, for instance on a memorable trip to Shanghai and Beijing, the White Room conversations – my continuing education – really mattered.

REFERENCES AND FOOTNOTES

—

About references

There are a some key project names and writings from Cedric Price Architects' earlier years in practice that appear consistently as references in a number of the ten contributors, texts and may be relevant to the later projects. Rather than repeatedly list them, a single reading list appears here followed by additional references for the more recent projects and the individual contributor essays. All project names and numbers appear in capitals throughout the book.

Suggested Reading List:

CEDRIC PRICE: WORKS II, Architectural Association, 1984, republished as CEDRIC PRICE: THE SQUARE BOOK, Wiley-Academy, 2003.

Royston Landau, New Directions in British Architecture, Georges Braziller, 1968 (includes FUN PALACE and POTTERIES THINKBELT).

Tom Porter, Architectural Drawing Master Class, Studio Vista, 1993.

Stanley Matthews, "Cedric Price and the architecture of 'Calculated Uncertainty: The Fun Palace and Potteries Thinkbelt", Doctoral dissertation, Columbia University, New York, 2001.

Key journals:

BUILDING DESIGN (BD) - columns between 1985 and 1990 (In-fill, Price Lists, Price Probes, Periscope, Closing Price).

ARCHITECT'S JOURNAL (AJ) - columns between July 1998 and September 1999 (Price Cuts).

AA FILES – no.8: obituary of R. Buckminster Fuller 1895-1983, no.19: Cedric Price Talks at the AA - a manifesto in the making, no.27: Engineers & Architects, Newby + Price, no.29: John Lyall, Welcoming Water – The City's Lung.

References for early iconic projects frequently referred to in text:

FUN PALACE
Peter Reyner Banham, "People's Palaces", New Statesman, 7 August 1964. Reyner Banham is extensively quoted on Cedric Price; this article is the most popular source on the Fun Palace. "The Fun Palace by Joan Littlewood, a statement by Cedric Price". New Scientist, 14 May 1964. The Architectural Review, January 1965.

POTTERIES THINKBELT
"Potteries Thinkbelt: A plan for an advanced educational industry in North Staffordshire", Architectural Design, October 1966. New Society, 2 June 1966.

GENERATOR
Building Design, 23 February 1979. Building Design , 9 November 1979. Architectural Review, January 1980. New Scientist, 19 March 1981.

INTER-ACTION CENTRE
Architectural Review, January 1973. New Statesman, 6 May 1977. Article by Cedric Price and B J Archer, Domus, April 1978.

Footnotes for introduction:

1   David Allford, The Creative Iconoclast, Cedric Price: Works II (AA), p.7.
2   Royston Landau, The Grove Dictionary of Art, ed. Jane Turner, Oxford University Press, 1996.
3   Reyner Banham, "People's Palaces", New Statesman, 7 August, 1964, reprinted in Reyner Banham, A Critic Writes, University of California Press, 1996 and C. Price, "Fun Palace", New Society, 15 April, 1965, No.133.
4   C. Price, "Potteries Thinkbelt", New Society, June 12, 1966. No.192.
5   Architectural Review, January 1973
6   "World's First Intelligent Building", RIBA Journal, London, June 1980, p63.
7   Royston Landau, New Directions in British Architecture, George Braziller.
8   Lecture delivered at the Architectural Association and the Bartlett Architecture School (University College London) December 1990.

9   Lecture delivered at the Architectural Association, 3 June 1994.
10 Carin Kuoni, Joseph Beuys, Kim Levin, Energy plan for Western Man – Joseph Beuys in America. (Four Walls Eight Windows 1993).
11 Another city for another life by Constant Nieuwenhuis, Internationale Situationniste #2, 1958.
12 Cedric Price - 2003.
13 SOUTH BANK.
14 Alistair McAlpine in ref to C. Price, Building, 16 August 1996.
15 Barnett Newman, The Artist-Critic in Barnett Newman, Selected Writings and Interviews, University of Calfornia Press, 1992.
16 taken from an obituary which appeared in The Pottery Gazette and Glass Trade Review, March 1943, of CP's uncle J.F. Price, designer of ceramics and President of the Society of Industrial Artists. The writer goes on to describe Jack Price as a "practical idealist" which seems an equally fitting description of nephew, Cedric.
17 William Wordsworth, "A Poet's Epitaph".

Additional for projects in main text:

Special Issue: Anticipatory Architecture: Cedric Price, AJ, 5 September 1996. This issue includes articles on Cedric Price Architects and covers a range of projects and themes included in this book, e.g, 198 STRATTON, 214 HAVEN, 205 RINK, 216 APPEX, 212 MILLS, 189/190 STRATE, 220 MAGNET, 180 WESTAL, 222 TASKFORCE.

Contributors' footnotes:

Robin Middleton (page 028)
1   John Summerson, Heavenly Mansions, 1949 (republished Norton 1998).
2   Le Corbusier, Maison Jaoul, Neuilly-sur-Seine, Paris, France, 1954 to 1956.
3   Joan Littlewood, Joan's Book, Methuen, 2003.
4   see FUN PALACE in main reading list.
5   see POTTERIES THINKBELT in main reading list.
6   Norbert Wiener, Cybernetics, or Control and Communication in the Animal and the Machine, MIT Press 1948, 1961.
7   by way of some recognition of his work, Cedric Price was awarded the Frederick Keisler Prize for Architecture and the Arts in Vienna, January 2003.

John Frazer (page 046)

1   Adrian Forty, **Words and Buildings –
    A Vocabulary of Modern Architecture**,
    Thames & Hudson, London, 2000.
2   Reyner Banham, "People's Palaces",
    New Statesman 68, 7 August 1964,
    reprinted in Reyner Banham,
    A Critic Writes: essays by Reyner Banham,
    University of California Press, LA, 1996.
3   Neil Spiller (ed) **Cyber-Reader**,
    Phaidon, London, 2002.
4   Peter Eisenman, "Post Functionalism"
    in Michael Hays (ed) **Architectural Theory
    since 1968**, Columbia University Press, 1998.
5   ibid.
6   Roy Landau, **New Directions in British
    Architecture**, Georges Braziller, 1968
7   Jenks & Baird (eds) **Meaning in Architecture**,
    Barrie & Rockliff, London, 1969.
8   "World's First Intelligent Building",
    RIBAJournal, London, June 1980, p 63.
9   Letter from John and Julia Frazer to
    Cedric Price, 1979.
10 Slide set, tape and booklet: Cedric Price,
    "Technology is the answer but what was the
    question?", Pidgeon Audio Visual, London.
11 Samantha Hardingham,
    email to John Frazer, May 2002.
12 Meeting with Cedric for breakfast at
    RIBA, 21 May 2002.
13 Cedric Price, AA Files 19,
    Architectural Association, London.
14 John Frazer, **An Evolutionary Architecture**,
    Architectural Association, London 1995.

Neil Spiller (page 049)

1   SEE THE SQUARE BOOK, main reading list
    Further reading: **Cyberreader** (ed) Neil Spiller,
    Phaidon 2002. Neil Spiller, **Digital Dreams –
    The Architecture of the New Alchemic
    Technologies**, Watson and Guptill 1998.
    "Reflexive Architecture", Architectural Design,
    (ed.) Neil Spiller, Wiley Academy, May 2002.
    Neil Spiller, "Architectural Education and
    Critical Paranoia", in Young Blood, Architectural
    Design, February 2001, (guest ed.) Neil Spiller,
    Wiley Academy 2001.

Kester Rattenbury (page 072)

1   see FUN PALACE in main reading list
2   Kester Rattenbury, "Builder of Bridges",
    The Guardian, July 5 1996, Arts, pp4-5.
3   Cedric Price was a regular or semi-regular
    columnist on BD in various capacities between
    1985 and 1990: In-fill 10 May 1986, p11,
    to 19 December 1986.
5   Closing Price; Price Lists, 7 September 1990.
    When Paul Finch left BD to edit (and later
    publish) AJ, Price's column switched
    ground too. Price Cuts ran in The Architects'
    Journal from July 1998 to September 1999.
5   See **Richard Rogers: The Complete Works**
    Volume 1, by Kenneth Powell, Phaidon 1999
    or **Richard Rogers**, a biography, by Brian
    Appleyard, Faber and Faber 1986.
    The Fun Palace is usually given as the key
    source, though more detailed sources also note
    the influence of Archigram, Oscar Nitzchke's
    Maison de la Publicité, and the input
    throughout of engineers, Arup, who originally
    proposed the moving floors and who were fully
    involved in the development of the project.
6   This argument is put by Rem Koolhaas in
    Re:CP, by Cedric Price, edited by Hans Ulrich
    Obrist, with contributions from Arata Isozaki,
    Patrick Keiller and Rem Koolhaas, seen in
    proof form prior to publication (August
    media/Birkhauser) in 2003.
7   (The scheme was tragically not the final
    winner - apparently, Philip Johnson said it
    wasn't socially viable - or, as Price more
    accurately put it, commercial enough.
    Price always challenged the over-development
    of New York and proposed this scheme
    in mitigation. Over-development of NY was
    traditionally seen as its greatest characteristic.
    One wonders would his scheme have won
    post 9/11. Since then over-development
    has arguably become more demonstrably
    contentious.)
8   **Re: CP** as before.

Jane Briginshaw (page 074)

1   Herbert Muschamp, "Critic's Notebook;
    Design Fantasies for a Strip of the West
    Side" New York Times, 18 October 1999.
    Cedric Price, Lunchtime lecture, reported
    in Building Design, March 1995.
2   see **THE SQUARE BOOK**, main reading list.
3   Cedric Price
4   Speech by David Miliband at the National
    Head Teachers Conference, Torquay,
    6 June 2002.
5   Building Design paraphrasing Cedric Price,
    BD, 24 May 1996 .
6   Article by Roy Hattersley, The Guardian,
    3 March 2003.

John Lyall (page 083)

1   Cedric Price, "The National Schools Plan",
    AJ, 25 May 1966.
2   The Archigram Group (est. early 1960s)
    comprising Peter Cook, David Greene,
    Warren Chalk, Mike Webb, Ron Herron and
    Dennis Crompton (www.archigram.net).
3   The CLASP System – a system of building
    developed in the 1950s which came out of the
    post-war tradition of co-operative research,
    experiment and development in architecture.
    It was based upon light-steel construction,
    adapted to combat the difficulties of sites liable
    to mining subsidence and also the earliest
    venture in bringing British local authorities
    together and pooling their resources to build
    more and better schools. Ref. Andrew Saint,
    **Towards a Social Architecture: The Role of
    School Building in Post-War England**, Yale
    University Press, 1987.
4   **Archigram Nine**, ed. Peter Cook,
    Archigram,1970.

Jude Kelly (page 086)

1   Reproduction of illustration in **Joan's Book**,
    The autobiography of Joan Littlewood,
    Methuen, 2003.

Simon Allford (page 088)

1   Cedric Price, "My Kind of Town",
    Architecture Today – no. 1.

Paul Finch (page 122)

1   Articles in **BD**- see main reading list.
2   Articles in **The AJ** - see main reading list.
3   Alistair McAlpine, **Memoirs - Once a Jolly
    Bagman**, Phoenix (Orion Books), 1998.
4   "This is Tomorrow", Whitechapel Art Gallery
    1956, iconic exhibition which explored
    architecture, technology, sci-fi and
    consumerism. Richard Hamilton's poster for
    the show, featuring a TV-age interior with
    body-builder is frequently cited as the
    founding moment of pop art.
5   The Architecture Club – established 1922,
    total membership approx. 400, of which half
    are architects.
6   Restaurant, St. John, St. John's Street,
    London EC1.